RODNEY
KING

Lawrence J. Spagnola

THE RIOT W

with

THE RIOT WITHIN

MY JOURNEY FROM REBELLION TO REDEMPTION

HarperOne

An Imprint of HarperCollinsPublishers

HarperOne

HarperCollins books may be purchased for educational, business, or sales promotional use. For information, please write: Special Markets Department, Harper-Collins Publishers, 10 East 53rd Street, New York, NY 10022.

HarperCollins website: http://www.harpercollins.com

HarperCollins®, 📖®, and HarperOne™
are trademarks of HarperCollins Publishers.

FIRST EDITION

Designed by Level C

Library of Congress Cataloging-in-Publication Data is available upon request.

ISBN 978–0–06–219443–5

12 13 14 15 16 RRD(H) 10 9 8 7 6 5 4 3 2 1

To the city of Los Angeles

CONTENTS

Chapter 1
THE WORLD WIDE OPEN

GROWING UP

"Who wants to go fishing?" Those were just the sweetest words to my seven-year-old ears, and had me out in Daddy's car with my rod and tackle before he was finished asking. Gailen, my older brother by a year, loved catching dinner too, but not as much as me. Fishing was my favorite thing to do. Wave good-bye to Momma, and off we went. Daddy knew all the good spots, and it didn't matter what was biting: pickerel, blue gills, carp, suckers, trout . . . just bring it. That was pure heaven.

They used to call my daddy Kingfish, which I thought was a pretty cool nickname. He was the best fisherman around. He taught me a lot of tricks about catching fish, fresh- and saltwater—the proper bait, lures, hooks, pound test, and everything.

Not far from where I was born, near my Grammy Rosetta's home up in Northern California, were miles and miles of these open irrigation canals that wound in and around the Sacramento River. These canals were used to get water to the field—crops and melons in that area. Somehow fish would get into these waterways. It wasn't like shooting fish in a barrel, but it was close. We would drive up this dirt run called One Mile Road and do a lot of fishing up there during summer vacation.

Some days, though, the fish would not bite no matter what, like they just wanted to spite you. One time, we tried every spot and every bait, but after four hours, nothing. Kingfish was so fed up, he opened up a valve for the floodgate that divided one of those canals and drained off about a hundred yards of ditch, just like that.

Gailen's and my jaws dropped, because suddenly we were looking out over a dozen fish just flopping around in the mud. Daddy laughed and yelled, "What're you waiting for? Go get 'em!" My brother and I never had so much fun, ankle deep in mud, grabbing mostly suckers and tossing them up on the bank for Dad to stuff into a canvas bag.

But that's not why that day is etched in my mind. It was because my leg got stuck at one point and made a funny suction sound when I tried to pull myself out of the ditch. I was laughing at first, but it felt like quicksand, pulling me down the more I struggled. I began to panic and started yelling for help because I was just a runt and had lost sight of Dad and Gailen. I went from shouting to screaming pretty fast, because when you're a kid, your imagination can get the best of you, and I started thinking about what would happen if I got sucked underground before anyone could get a fix on me. This big ole catfish was only about three feet away from me, stuck on the bank. Catfish are incredibly durable and can breathe for a bit out of water. He was staring me down with this sad look that said, "Yer a goner, just like me."

All of a sudden I heard yelling, but it wasn't my dad, and it wasn't Gailen. "Who is that? Who's there?!" I screamed at the top of my lungs, really panicked. Yanking and yelling, yelling and yanking. I almost dislocated my leg at the knee trying to rip it out of that stinky mud with one mighty pull. But without anything to brace against, it was hopeless.

Next thing I heard was "Hush up, boy! Can't you hear that farmer yelling? The whole valley must a heard you!" Then Dad's arm wrapped around my waist like a steel cable and pulled me out of that muck easy as a greased pole. He tucked me under his arm and carried me on a dead run to get away from that farmer who was gonna be real sore once he saw we emptied one of his ditches. I saw Gailen just ahead, jumping into the car. Daddy tossed me and the bag of fish in the back seat, and we lit out of there. All the time that farmer was howling away.

RUN, NIGGER!

Fishing was one of the ways we had fun in the water. But that was only when Dad felt like it. Swimming was by far the thing to do every day of the summer. Whether we were visiting my family up in Sacramento or at home in Altadena, me and my brothers would always end up at the local water hole. At home, the best swimming was near Devil's Gate Dam, where we'd splash around all day. Gailen, who was about six at the time, would lead us down there. Mom wasn't crazy about us going swimming and made us promise to keep an eye on our little brother, Juan, because he was still pretty young. There were always other kids down there, big and small, from all parts of Altadena and Pasadena. We were just keeping cool in the hot sun, messing around skipping stones and playing tag off this old, half-sunk wooden raft.

I was a pretty good swimmer and could stay in the water forever. One day I was just bobbing up and down, trying to touch bottom. I could actually get a good rhythm going and found that the further I popped up out of the water, the better my momentum to slice down and get my toes into that cold muck below. That was such a cool feeling, and there were only a few of us who could touch bottom at the deepest part.

As my head broke the surface for the umpteenth time, this object flew past my face, missing me by inches. My eyes were still closed, but from the sound of the *ker-plunk* it made when it hit the surface of the water, I was shocked to realize it must've been a pretty decent-sized rock. I was about to yell, "Quit it!" when another one buzzed by, this time just over my head. I suddenly felt very exposed and helpless, and was never more frightened in my life. I surface dived and swam to the shore underwater almost the whole way, then clambered up the bank. There were stones flying everywhere, and I could hear yelling from my other brothers. As I sprinted up the path to get away, I could hear yelling from the other kids. Then I heard it for the first time in my life: "Run, nigger!"

What? But I did. I must have been on a dead run for a

thousand yards before I dared look behind me. I figured I'd see all the kids that were being pelted by rocks sprinting right behind me. I swore that if Gailen had been in on this sick game, then Mom *and* Dad were going to hear about it. Gailen was only a year older than me, but he was a lot bigger than me, and I got real angry as I imagined him laughing at me. I was confused when I finally stopped, because there weren't any other kids in sight. I was tempted to go back, but the thought of rocks whizzin' by my head kept me away.

It wasn't until I was heading back home that I ran into Gailen and Juan. They were both crying, particularly Juan, who was nearly hysterical. Gailen came right up to me, and I could see he was angry. "Where did you go? Why did you take off on us? They wanted to kill us. That big redhead was gonna tie me up with a rope he had wrapped around a big rock, but Juan came right up to him and threw sand in his face. He was screaming he was gonna kill us, but we took off before his friends could catch us."

I didn't know what to say, and I felt so awful when I realized I had abandoned my brothers. Gailen told me how all the white kids ganged up on us without any warning. I had no idea what Gailen was talking about. Up until that point in my life, I had no real grasp of white kids, black kids, or blue kids. We were all just kids, as far as I could tell.

I can still see the look on Momma's face when Gailen told her what happened, and her expression when she looked at me after Gailen told her what I did. Her disapproving glance was only there for a second, but it cut right through my heart.

Mom softened her look right away, but I had seen it, and it was devastating to me. I just wanted to roll up in a ball and die right there. Juan couldn't even look at me. I think he was embarrassed for me because his heart was so pure, he probably couldn't even process the idea of me leaving my brothers in a situation where they could get hurt.

END OF INNOCENCE

That was the day that I learned what the word *nigger* meant. Even though we were all just kids that loved swimming, running, hanging out, and playing games, we were not the same. I had been down at the waterhole many times and never noticed anything different between my brothers and me and all the rest of the children. We were kids, and that was it. Now it turned out that because we had different hair and darker skin, the kids with the lighter skin didn't like playing with us. I loved the way I looked, the way my body sucked up the sunshine, the way my hair dried off with a shake. It wasn't like I didn't see there was different shades to us kids. I even felt sorry for some of those pasty-faced children and how they'd get all red and burned until their skin figured it out.

What happened that day made no sense to me. I could not understand what the big fuss was about. But I did know that I felt real bad for leaving my brothers, and it didn't help to have Gailen ask, "Why did you take off on us?" every five minutes. I might have understood if the other kids got mad at us because me and my brothers were faster, or always won at tag, or hogged the raft, but that wasn't the case. So I was hurt but still pretty clueless. I vividly remember that feeling of confused innocence.

Maybe every black kid can think back to the day when the whole world changed and they had to have who they were and why that was different explained to them. That was one sad day, and we need to dedicate ourselves to removing that day from every black kid's calendar forever.

Children are color blind by nature, and it is a very tragic day when that truth changes. I have been asked what I recommend when it comes to us building a less racist, more peace-loving world, and the one thing I'd promote over any other is greater integration. Encourage situations where young people spend more time with each other—in schools, camps, playgrounds, churches, lunchrooms, and living rooms. The longer our children are color blind, the better they will all get along, even after they realize that there are grown-ups that make way too big a deal about our appearance. Let kids find that absurd, and laugh at the fools who try to create bad feelings between children with different skin, hair, and eyes.

DAD'S GIRLFRIEND

One Saturday, me, Daddy, and Gailen didn't get to the fishing hole until late afternoon. Daddy detoured over to that lady's house who lived on a hill. I saw her once. She was light skinned with frizzy hair and didn't look at all like Momma. Daddy just parked on the dead-end street and told us, "Wait in the car."

We knew better than to get out of that car. But after an hour or so, we was all frisky, like a couple of trapped badgers. So me and Gailen killed time wrestling in the backseat. All the while, though, I kept having this strange feeling in my chest, all tight like I couldn't breathe right. Gailen thought I was getting some kind of asthma attack, but it wasn't that. It wasn't that at all. I always got this tightness when something was bugging me deep down. Problem was, I had no idea what was bothering me that day.

We got tired of wrestling, so we switched to working that backseat. Man, we'd rock that old Buick up and down, back and forth till we almost bust the springs. We'd shove our elbows into the upholstery and go nuts, but eventually we got tired of rocking the car too.

I jumped up in the front seat to play fighter pilot with the steering wheel and gearshift. Gailen told me to stop messin' or Daddy would beat us both. But I was having a good time—it took my mind off us not getting to fish. How long was Daddy going to be, anyways?

Suddenly I heard the weirdest clank sound, like the tooth on a gear breaking or something. Next thing I knew, the car started rolling, slow like, but definitely moving. Trouble was, the street ended in a cement culvert that dropped suddenly about ten, fifteen feet down to a drainage ditch. If the car went over, we'd be messed up pretty good.

The same moment I heard that metallic sound, my dad must have come out of the house, because I heard him yell. I looked over, and I never saw anyone move so fast. He ran across two front lawns and grabbed the driver's side door handle just as the car was gaining speed. He opened that door and shoved me over like I was a fly. Daddy hit the brake and stopped the car a couple feet short of the drop-off.

Gailen let out a tiny whistle, and I just sat frozen, watching Daddy stare at his white knuckles on the steering wheel. Years later, thinking back on this, I've got to admit it was pretty cool seeing the old man in action, even though he'd probably had his fill of action already that day.

We didn't catch but two fish that afternoon, so on the way home, Daddy stopped and got some groceries. He didn't say much when he got back in the car, and I was too worried about getting a beating to be sad about the fact that we didn't get in much fishing.

DAD'S BEATINGS

I knew I was in trouble, just by how quiet Daddy was on the way home. I was just praying he wasn't mad enough to use the extension cord on me. That was the worst. Most times he used his belt or a razor strap, and that hurt something awful, but because it was wide, it wasn't too terrible.

The absolute worst was when he'd go upstairs and run the bathwater, then come down and say, "Go on up there, strip, and get yourself soaking wet . . . and don't dry off." Man, I'd start crying before I even got out of the tub, knowing what was coming. That thin extension cord on my wet skin was just the worst. Pain like you just want to die and get it over with. The first time Daddy whipped me that way, he'd been drinking. He'd always swing harder when he was drunk. Well that extension cord came across the back of my thigh and I'd scream, almost passing out from the pain.

I'd get the worst damn welts on my legs, arms, and back. Big-ass raised marks, a quarter-inch high, all up and down. Momma put Vaseline on them to help them heal, because you didn't want the welts to dry out and crack. Then they'd take forever to get better. I used to run my fingers over those welts all the time, because as they healed, they started to itch something awful. Teachers were always telling me to sit still, but those welts made it almost impossible.

Me and my three brothers were pretty wild, so I guess we had it coming most of the time. But sometimes I couldn't sleep right for a couple nights, tossing and turning, just couldn't find a comfortable spot. Then I'd be so tired in school the next day.

Even when Dad didn't hit us, he still had us exhausted for school. When I was eight, Dad got the idea to take Gailen and me along on his night shift custodial work up at the medical center on Green Street in Pasadena. Momma didn't like it, but I guess she had to pick her battles with Daddy, caused he'd shove her around pretty hard, although I never saw him hit Momma. She had one rule when he beat us: "Not on the face!" She'd get awful upset if his aim was off and he caught us one in the head.

So we'd get to the medical center around seven o'clock in the evening, and Daddy would have us cleaning and waxing them floors every damn night. He always had a bottle with him, and a radio. He'd sit down and say, "Get to work." Then he'd turn on that damn radio and play nothing but country music. Johnny Cash, Merle Haggard, Buck Owens, Willie Nelson—all them old-time country crackers. Gailen and I used to just shake our heads. Gailen would say, "We got the only niggadaddy in L.A. listenin' to country music, and that's a fact."

He must have got a hankering for country from his other job, which was cleaning white folks' houses with Momma during the day. We figured he was listening to what the white people were listening to in Altadena and Pasadena, and it sank in and caught on.

Me and Gailen got good at working the buffers, raising them tiles to a high shine. The place was huge, so we'd need the whole shift to finish up. We'd be running those buffers nonstop until two A.M. Then Daddy would punch out. By the time we got home and in bed, it would seem like we'd only get an hour's sleep before we had to get up for school.

In class, all I'd want to do was put my head down. I couldn't concentrate, and my face felt hot all the time. Information just wasn't going in. Over time, the teachers decided I was slow and called in Momma to talk about what to do.

They told Momma I wasn't taking things in the way a normal student is supposed to. Said that right in front of me. I wish I'd had the guts to defend myself. I know this is going to sound pathetic, but I was just too damn tired to raise much of a fuss. And anyway, if I said something about Daddy, there could be hell to pay at home.

Holding me back a year wasn't an option, because my momma pointed out they had already done that to me in first grade, though I don't know why. So they decided to put me in a class for special kids. They told me I was going to be put in with the mentally retarded children. I was a little scared, but also a little relieved, thinking maybe now school would be easier. Kids are always looking for an easy way out, and I guess I had found mine.

They called it L.D.G. for Learning Disabled Group, but the kids used to say it stood for Little Dumb Guy, and I hated that. I was so embarrassed the first time they made me take the short bus to school. I begged the driver to drop us off around the side of the school so my friends wouldn't see me getting off with all the slow kids. The school kids would point at us and make fun.

That made me feel terrible, kind of worthless, like I wasn't a normal kid. I was a defective, broken boy. The first couple days, I cried and cried when I got home. And it got worse, because getting stuck in special ed meant I also wasn't permitted to play sports for my school. I loved playing baseball and was pretty good at it.

PREDATORS

One of the teachers, Mr. Robert E. Jones, a really bright, popular gay man who taught social sciences at John Muir High School, knew how badly I wanted to play baseball. Well he went to bat for me, spoke up for me with the officials for the school league, and got me on my school's baseball team.

It was one of the happiest moments of my life. I felt normal again, like I belonged, and my teammates were real cool with me and fun to be around. We weren't the best team—in fact, we were probably a little below average when it came to wins and losses, but we all loved getting out there on the field. That feeling of sliding into bases, slapping the dirt off your uniform and pulling for one another is just the best feeling in the world. Baseball saved me.

I remember Mr. Jones was very excited I was playing sports, and he kept saying we had to go out and celebrate. I still needed a glove and cleats before I could start practicing. He told me to swing by his classroom after school and we'd figure something out. Well, by that point, Mr. Jones could do no wrong in my book. I even had a little fantasy of him having a brand-new glove waiting for me when I stopped by his classroom.

Mr. Jones had a fantasy too. He asked me to sit down when I walked in. I'd never seen someone so glad to see me. Then he sat down right in front of me. He started asking me what I liked about baseball, what my favorite position was, and if I could run fast. I noticed he got a big kick out of whatever I said, and kept slapping his lap as he was laughing. Then he switched to slapping my lap, and laughing even harder. He asked me about my favorite ice cream flavor, and after another round of laughing, I noticed he just left his hand on my thigh.

Now, if it hadn't been for my brother Juan and an experience he had with a coach, I'm not sure how it would have played out for me that day with Mr. Jones. Juan was a real good athlete, the back-up quarterback on the football team. This coach used to wear real tight pants, and I knew my brother and the other football players used to mock the hell out of him behind his back.

Well, one day the coach got so fed up that he locked Juan, another player, and himself in the equipment room and yelled at them for making fun of him. Juan said he laughed out loud, but only because he was nervous. Well, Coach didn't really get mad, but he started chasing them around. Juan wasn't sure if it was to play grab ass or if he really wanted to hurt them, but Juan wasn't going to hang around to find out. He was able to kick the door open, and got out of there real fast. The other kid took off right behind him.

That story rung up loud and clear in my head soon as Mr. Jones's big old hand started squeezing my thigh. I didn't push it off, but I must have made an odd look because suddenly Mr. Jones said, "You okay, Rodney?" And I said, "I'm good. I'm good." Then he squeezed again and started working his hand up a little farther. That's when I knew I'd had enough and shot up out of that seat and stood, saying way too loud, "I'm good, real good." But I didn't run, at least I don't *remember* running. I felt frozen to that spot, unable to move away. Mr. Jones was my friend who had stuck up for me. In my mind, Mr. Jones looked genuinely concerned because we were celebrating and I was ruining it acting all fidgety.

I'd like to think I took my cue from Juan and got out of the room as fast as I could, but for the life of me, I cannot remember anything else until I got back home. It's all a blank—but maybe that's just as well.

TRAGEDY

Unfortunately, it makes me upset every time I think about Mr. Jones because years later, in 1986, another student from our school, Robert Butler, came over to Mr. Jones's house late at night and walked in through an unlocked back door. He woke Mr. Jones and complained that the teacher had stopped communicating with him. Jones said he was real tired and asked if they could talk about it in the morning.

But something inside Butler snapped when the teacher rolled over and went back to sleep. He got Jones's gun that he kept in an ice bucket in another part of the house, came back, and pumped two bullets into the sleeping teacher. Then he went into the living room where a seventeen-year-old student, Ronald McClendon, was crashed out on the couch and shot him too. McClendon was a pretty popular JV basketball player at Muir High School, and Jones was a well-loved teacher. It was a major shock to everyone, a catastrophe of unbelievable proportions.

After his death, it got out that Jones had offered troubled male students a place to live over the years, and may have admitted to some that he was gay. It makes me think about all the trouble that's come out recently at Penn State and Syracuse University. There's a lot of secrets out there, and a lot of unhappy people who use their authority to prey on others.

We had predators in my own family. We had a crazy-ass female cousin who was about thirteen years old when I was about five. She developed real early and was pretty much a woman by then. She would come over to our house to babysit, and do the sickest things, although to us it was just games, but we didn't like playing with her.

She'd strip down and try to get my brothers to play along with her. She'd make up some reason for having to do "inspections" and said these were grown-up games for big boys and that we were old enough to play them now. But Gailen and I squirmed and wiggled our way out of the bedroom. She'd laugh and tackle us, rubbing us all over. We didn't know what to call what she was doing; we just knew it made us feel funny inside.

She sat us down and told us she would beat us up real bad if we said anything to Momma. My brothers and I have tried to forgive my cousin for what she did, and since she has apologized like a thousand times for what we would all like to forget, then it's best to forgive.

PHYSICAL ASSAULT

I have been asked countless times if I've forgiven those officers for beating me. The short answer is yes. The long answer is that I work on it every day, and every day I let it go a little more. I know I did wrong that night, and I believe they did wrong too, but we all have to move on and let go of the hate.

Hate is the worst. The first person I ever hated was my father. I hated him for the way he beat us, for the way he pushed my mother around, and for what he made us do. When I think back, Gailen always stuck up for my father, and I always sided with Momma even if it meant I'd be getting a whipping for it. There didn't seem to be any reason for Gailen to always be on Dad's side, but he was.

I think about my father making us work that night job, and the negative effect it had on my education. But I guess it was just Daddy's way of holding down more than one job. I just wish I hadn't wasted all that time buffing and waxing when I could have been reading and writing.

Not long ago I visited the place where we worked, and wouldn't you know, one of the janitors there told me they had just put in new linoleum less than a year earlier. He didn't remember my dad, but it wasn't like Dad did much socializing when he was working there. Most nights Daddy would just fall asleep and we'd have to wake him up to go home. He'd always be in a foul mood, and we were careful not to do anything to get him mad.

One time a wise-ass neighborhood kid, about nine years old, mouthed off to my dad after he told this punk to get off our property. I think that the kid rode his bike over our flowers or something. Well this boy just stared down Kingfish and told him to fuck off. I don't think it would have been such a big deal, but my dad's massive friend James was there, all six feet nine inches of him, and he heard what the kid said. James shook his head and said Dad needed to wake his boys up. So Dad went and told Gailen, who was eight, to teach the punk a lesson for talking that way to his elders.

Well, Gailen charged in kind of wide-eyed and wild. It looked pretty good for about five seconds, and then this kid proceeded to beat the royal crap out of my brother. Gailen lasted maybe a minute. This kid was lightning fast and ruthless. It hurt me just to watch poor Gailen, who was crying through two eyes that were quickly swelling shut. Gailen and my dad were close, so it must have destroyed Gailen to let the old man down like that.

Then Dad looked at me and said, "Get on in there!" Well I stepped in, but my heart wasn't in it. Particularly since I'd just seen my big brother get beaten. I hate that feeling when you're about to do something and you're just not into it. You wonder, "What am I doing? This is really stupid!" Then you do it anyway.

I lasted about twenty seconds. I got in one swing and then *wham*—he hit me about fifteen times and my legs just buckled. It was so embarrassing. This kid looked at us like we were nothing and took off. I was scared over what Dad was going to do to us for getting beaten, because things had to be just right with him, or look out.

Just like those linoleum floors four A.M.—they had to look perfect or else he'd let us have it. When me and Gailen got older, though, we could really take a whooping from Dad and barely cry. Our eyes would get wet is all. Gailen used to stare Kingfish down, and I think it kind of scared the old man. We had actually gotten used to the extension cord whippings, which was the worst pain. Learned to just shrug it off. Fuck that old drunk, anyway.

THE LAST BEATING

I figure that's why all the kicking, Taser zaps, and baton blows didn't really keep me down when the cops were beating me in 1991. It was a tolerable level of pain that I had felt plenty of times before, that's for sure. Even when they'd catch me right on the joint (like they're trained), bust my wrist or elbow or knee, it wasn't enough to keep me down. I didn't even notice my ankle was broke until they told me. It just wasn't working right, was all I noticed that night.

And when they busted up my face, fractured my eye socket and all, I was more worried about Momma seeing me, cause I hate when she gets upset. "What did you do now?" I can still hear her saying that as I was growing up. Anytime I'd get in trouble and she'd catch wind of it: "What did you do now?"

The worst was when she heard the cops saying I had to be on PCP and I wasn't. It really bothered me when they told the press I must have been doing angel dust to act the way I did. I had never touched the stuff, and the doctors didn't find a damn trace of it in my body. I really hated them for saying that. But the damage had been done. Once they uttered those words, people were going to think that, no matter what. But I try not to waste my time hating anymore.

MOMMA KNOWS

Momma says that Jehovah will have his day of reckoning with people, and I believe that. She says that there will be an accounting the likes of which we cannot even begin to imagine. The wrath of God will descend upon us with fury, and the Day of Judgment will be swift. God is just, and we will be held responsible for every blessed action, for every sin that we have ever committed.

That's why I feel there is no sense in being consumed by hatred. Those who have done wrong will be punished. In the meantime, I have found it much more bearable and productive to try to forgive.

I believe that hate is the most powerful, destructive emotion. It deadens our spirit and drives the soul into darkness. For many years I fostered an intense hatred, and it was one of the factors that created a riot within me. I could never quell the chaos that reigned inside, nor did I even want to.

I feared that freeing myself from hatred would lead to my becoming soft and vulnerable. That vulnerability would certainly lead to my destruction. As a young black man, I could never drop my guard. I'd rather hate than be hurt, and whenever I was tempted to forgive and forget, I'd just reread a passage by the Trappist monk Thomas Merton. I found Merton's quote about Harlem in Eldridge Cleaver's *Soul On Ice,* the powerful book Cleaver wrote while he was in jail:

Here in this huge, dark, steaming slum, hundreds of thousands of Negroes are herded together like cattle, most of them with nothing to eat and nothing to do. All the senses and imagination and sensibilities and emotions and sorrows and desires and hopes and ideas of a race with vivid feelings and deep emotional reactions are forced in upon themselves, bound inward by an iron ring of frustration: the prejudice that hems them in with its four insurmountable walls. In this huge cauldron, inestimable natural gifts, wisdom, love, music, science, poetry are stamped down and left to boil with the dregs of the elementally corrupted nature, and thousands upon thousands of souls are destroyed by vice and misery and degradation, obliterated, wiped out, washed from the register of the living, dehumanized.

What has not been devoured, in your dark furnace, Harlem, by marijuana, by gin, by insanity, hysteria, syphilis?

Those words got my blood boiling, and I could have stayed locked in a state of hatred for the rest of my life. But age and experience change a man, and finally, after a lot of painful lessons, I accepted that we should let go of the loathing, but not the lesson.

CRIPS, BLOODS, AND BOOZE

Now, it's easy to talk about forgiveness, but honestly, to forgive and move on took plenty of effort on my part. When I was young and beat down by all the injustices I perceived, anger just festered naturally. Growing up, hate was all around me. I remember the intense turf battles that sprung up between the Bloods and Blues (Crips). I wasn't even aware of it at first, because I didn't think of a certain area as being Blood territory. It was just Jackie Robinson Park, one of the neighborhood playgrounds where I used to hang out.

Me and a few friends worked at McDonald's for long hours and low pay. I worked the late shift, then had to clean the entire place top to bottom before I could close up for the night around two A.M. I'd always head out hoping that I could catch up with my friends. We'd usually gather at one of a half dozen construction sites in the northern part of Altadena.

The first time I drank alcohol at age eleven, it felt like someone threw a switch in the back of my head. Usually everyone has to get a little used to the taste of beer, but not me. I loved it right from the start. I said to myself, "This stuff is amazing. It's so delicious." And I was immediately hooked.

I turned into the person I always wanted to be after that first quart of beer. I was happy, witty, confident, and ready to make the men laugh and the ladies love. I had the disease in me, just like my dad, but I was nowhere near realizing that or even remotely fearing that anything negative could ever come of alcohol. I loved to drink from the start.

Now I know what my dad went through, because I have prowled the dark side and have paid dearly for my addiction to alcohol, which I feel is the most dangerous drug. Not the worst drug, like meth or heroin, but the one that wrecks the most lives because it's totally legal, easily accessible, and a stone-cold killer. My dad didn't make it past forty-two.

Weed came my way about the same age, and that brought on a much mellower scene. We had us some tasty chronic in my day. Seemed like every bag of weed back then was primo. I'd go back and forth between which I liked more—weed or booze. But weed was better than beer while listening to music. Nothing beat some tasty bud and a fine groove. That was the best time, smoking and cranking tunes at some empty, half-built house.

And even though I was only eleven, I had me a mini bike to get around, anywhere I wanted to go. I quickly graduated to a Honda 354. At thirteen I got my first car, a 1964 Chevy station wagon. You could get a permit back then at a pretty young age, but I didn't bother. Mom didn't like that I had wheels and was driving around underage and all, but it didn't bother Dad in the least. Something in him liked it.

This was a pretty carefree time in my life, and I was completely unaware of the hate that was dividing my hometown and the rest of L.A. On the first day of junior high school, I plopped down into one of the back seats in homeroom without a second thought. This scrawny, pimply black kid said I was in the wrong seat, that them back seats were for some other guys. I just laughed and kind of ignored him. That turned out to be a big mistake.

Turned out those back-row seats were reserved for the ABCs—the Altadena Black Crips, and they were not to be messed with. They would beat you, put you in the hospital, if you crossed them in any way. Trouble was, they had all kinds of rules and restrictions, and most of the time, you didn't know when you were breaking them. But that time they told me straight out they were going to be waiting for me after school, saying I was going to have to pay for what I did.

Soon as I walked out of school that day, they followed me to this Jack in the Box parking lot where one of them hit me with a stick. I panicked and ran as fast as I could. Six or seven guys started chasing me, so I ducked into some horse stables that sat off the road. The stables doubled as a bookie joint, and I just holed up in there on instinct, knowing there would definitely be some men in there that I could hide behind, men that might know me because I was a local.

I was scared but wasn't going to say a thing. No way would I rat anyone out, but I definitely wasn't leaving that place until it was safe. After a bit, one of the bettors figured out what was happening, why I was pacing around. This guy was a cool, white man who was manager of a small grocery store near our home. He liked me for some reason, and walked me outside. The ABCs had gotten bored and were gone by then. I was lucky because kids were getting killed every week, with Pasadena becoming turf for the Bloods and Altadena being mostly Crip territory.

Of all my three brothers, Gailen was the only one who dipped into the whole Crips thing, but he never went real deep. The rest of us sort of had a free pass to travel around Altadena and Pasadena without incident. As long as we didn't trip any wires, we were cool on either turf because we had grown up in the area and were known to most everyone as locals.

In fact, we got away with doing things that the gang would never have allowed anyone else to do without paying some kind of tribute. When the Rose Bowl Parade rolled down Colorado Boulevard in Pasadena every New Year's Day, my brothers and me used to clean up. We figured out that we could valet cars for families that wanted to drive up real close—where they could get a good spot to see the parade. They would hand Gailen, Paul, Juan, or me the keys, and we would make a killing every New Year parking cars, but we had to hustle.

I remember actually earning some respect from one of the gang bangers for thinking it all up. We'd usually get twenty-five dollars a car and up to fifty dollars for an RV. Of course, if some out-of-state family had driven hundreds of miles to see the parade and could only afford fifteen or ten bucks, then that was cool, but we'd always start by asking for twenty-five. Eventually the city caught on and started bringing in professional valet services who would pay a hefty municipal fee to get in on the action.

But by then, I had moved on making extra money with a tree-cutting business that I started for myself after saving up enough to buy a '69 Ford pickup. It was all about having work that kept me outdoors. I loved trimming hedges, pruning trees, cutting dead limbs, and it didn't even feel like work. Those were great times when anything seemed possible. Sure, we'd still get a beating from Dad every now and then, and sometimes things weren't great at home, but I had a car, money, and girlfriends—and nobody, not even them Rockefellers, had it better. Life was just wide open.

Chapter 2

CHAOS WITHIN, CHAOS WITHOUT

DANCE WITH THE DEVIL

Whether it was working the Rose Bowl or pruning rose bushes, being outside working all day always made me build up a powerful appetite. Food just tastes better when you're real hungry, and nothing was more delicious than a home-cooked meal after a long, hard day in the fresh air. This was when I began a routine that seemed innocent enough at the time—but it quickly became my dance with the devil. It started with me picking up a couple forties of malt liquor on the way home. Nothing cut the thirst and went down better, especially after a hot afternoon of sawing branches and hauling wood in my pickup. It's common knowledge that malt beer has a higher alcohol content than regular lagers, but I drank it because I liked the taste. It was a little less sweet than a regular beer, and did a great job of washing away all that dust and grit in my mouth.

Now that's just plain, pathetic alcoholic talk right there, but you would have been hard pressed to convince me of that at the time. Being a drunk sneaks up on you, and pretty soon you don't even need that meal as much as another forty. Long before Red Bull there was just the Bull—Schlitz Malt Liquor. They had those fun commercials with Kool and The Gang, The Drifters, and Average White Band: "Don't say beer, say Bull." And I did because I loved the way it put me in a happy mood and seemed to make my troubles shut down for a while. Any problems I was having at the time—needing a new transmission for the truck, behind in payments, not getting enough work to keep me busy—all seemed to fall away. Not lining up enough work was the worst, and what they say about idle hands being the devil's workshop is absolutely true.

Maybe if I had been a more religious person, I would have seen the danger signs sneaking up on me. My mother, her sister, and some of their children embraced the Jehovah's Witness religion. Jehovah's Witnesses were big into door-to-door converting and preaching, and they were always handing out this book called *The Watchtower,* which I guess sums up all the things they believe in. It's important to follow everything they preach to the letter because they do this thing called shunning, where their members who don't follow the rules exactly are put on the outs until they repent.

I didn't like the idea that they don't believe we have immortal souls. They also don't believe in the existence of hell, although I wish there wasn't one. They don't have any need for Christmas, Easter, or birthdays—and that's just wrong. But the thing that threw me off the most about their teachings is their considering everyone else in society to be evil and influenced by the devil, so they avoid them. Seemed it was all about a strict belief in the Bible and nothing else, and best to live only among Jehovah's Witnesses and stay away from the immoral, corrupt rest of mankind.

Of course when I spoke with my mother about her faith as a Jehovah's Witness, I could see how their emphasis on socializing with like believers and the upholding of strict Christian values had attracted her. My mother eventually left my father, and I'm sure some of it had to do with the Jehovah Witnesses' complete rejection of physical abuse, failing to support one's family, and what they term the endangerment of spirituality. Those three points became the religion's approved grounds for legal separation, and Dad was definitely on what I'd call their version of the three strikes law. My parents truly loved each other, however, and did find a way to remarry before Dad died. Personally, I'm glad they did find a lasting love and peace between them. I know that as a kid, I used to smile and even get a little embarrassed when I saw my parents kiss, but it was a nice warm feeling all the same. Long after my parents quit making love, they were still in love.

Dad was never a Jehovah's Witness, but they knew him through my mom, and there were plenty of times he was in their presence. They must have built up a lot of respect for my father, because when he passed away, they dedicated a moment of prayer for him and had his portrait up on a screen. It wasn't a memorial service, but it was a nice commemoration.

I will say this about my father: he was well liked because he always had an upbeat, cheerful approach to life. He greeted people with a warm hello and always smiled when he walked down the street. I think the neighbors, his workmates, his friends—everyone—knew that Kingfish was a happy, easygoing, positive guy to be around. He told me that being an optimistic, friendly guy paid back big dividends. He told me one time, when the cleaning service he worked for had to let go of two people, that he wasn't that worried. He knew he had a solid relationship with his boss, who enjoyed my dad's company. My dad told me to try to be someone people like being around, someone people look forward to seeing. He convinced us kids that this made for fewer hassles as you go through life.

The Jehovah's Witnesses were pretty strict about love and marriage. They made any sex outside of the union reason for getting kicked out. They hate on homosexuals and same-sex marriages, and consider abortion to be murder, plain and simple. I could never be a Jehovah's Witness because my mom made it clear that gambling, drunkenness, illegal drugs, and smoking were out. I wasn't much of a gambler, but the thought of quitting some of those other things was too much.

The one thing I should have followed was their insistence that people only drink in moderation, because soon my idea of a couple beers to cut my thirst turned into a daily exercise to bury my blues. And the more I drank, the more I wanted. Suddenly, I wasn't getting enough outdoor jobs to keep up—and, even worse, I was late or completely forgetting the appointments that I did make.

Over the years, the drinking became much more damaging. At first, I'd skip school because I had a tree-cutting job all set up, but then I'd oversleep. Missing work really bothered me, but not getting to classes was no big deal. I'd had enough of school by then. I was never good at reading and math, and by the beginning of my senior year, I just let it go. I spent the rest of the year hanging out with my neighborhood friends, and then I married Denetta, who I called Dede, just before my class graduated.

That was also around the time, at age eighteen, that I entered the system by getting arrested and convicted for reckless driving. I was sentenced to eighty-four hours of community service. Yes, I popped my rap sheet cherry, like thousands of other Angelenos, while driving my car.

BAD TO WORSE

I could always scratch up enough coin to keep drinking, and the next decade continued to mess with my common sense and judgment. It all led to me deciding to head down to Marina del Rey on November 3, 1989, with my fishing rod. I was the provider in our house, and there wasn't anything left to feed my family, so I was going to do what I loved and had done many times before: I was going to catch us a nice fish dinner. Besides, I needed the time to just sit and think things through. How had everything gotten so messed up that suddenly I was broke with no jobs lined up?

I remember that day very well because I found a real good spot for casting on the break wall in Marina del Rey. There was even a raised slab of rock to sit up against. I settled in and popped a forty, ready to reel in some tasty halibut and rock cod, maybe even some ocean perch. My family was going to sit down to a feast tonight. Soon the offshore breeze picked up a bit, and that meant I had to recast more often. But that's fishing, and every day is different and beautiful.

It's a shame what's happened down there at the Marina. I used to catch twenty-inch and bigger halibut regularly, but that was because we followed an honor code at the Marina. Anything under a foot and a half got tossed back. And everyone did it. But the next wave of fishermen down there didn't give a shit about that stuff, and they kept everything they caught regardless of the size. I've seen them do it—throw five-inch babies in their basket and cart everything away. There's nothing left down there now—it's all fished out. Fishing is just as much about what you don't take as what you do. But to save the environment, you have to sacrifice, and that only comes from loving the land.

And here is where I get upset in the telling of this day in my life, because of what happens next. It was just plain unfair, lousy luck. But I've had plenty of that in my life—enough for five lifetimes. Anyway, that day I caught three beauties, one right after the other. And there was one big fish, twenty-two inches or longer, and heavy. When prepared right, halibut is one of the tastiest fish. Unfortunately, I lost one just as I was reeling it in close. The other two, I lay out on the flat rock next to me, I didn't take the extra time to clean them because I was excited and wanted to get that line back in the water while they was biting.

Well, about ten minutes later, I happened to notice the halibut weren't where I had laid them on the rock. What the . . . ?

I looked all around and, out of my peripheral vision, saw a big ole rat pulling part of my fish down into the cracks in the break wall rock. Damn! Well, I kind of shook my head and told myself I'd just catch three more. It doesn't take a genius to figure out what happened next. That's right. Nothing. I didn't catch another fish all afternoon. There were two other fishermen out there that day, and they both quit after a couple hours. But I hung tough. After a long afternoon, I had nothing but a sweaty T-shirt and a soaked butt to show for my efforts. The forties I'd drained left me feeling dehydrated, and as I worked my way across the break wall back to shore, I was hit with a pretty miserable feeling of desperation. I had gone from catching a feast to nothing. The rats were eating better than my family was. There was no way I was going back home empty-handed. I wasn't actually saying that to myself, but deep down, I was feeling it. No way.

Yet that's just what was happening, driving back home empty-handed with my mind racing and my stomach growling, a bad combination. I couldn't take it, I needed something to calm myself down, so I got off the highway around Monterey Park, completely parched, and looked for a grocery store. Monterey Park is a mostly Asian suburb to the east of downtown Los Angeles. I found a parking spot about a half block from a little corner convenience store. I walked by and noticed there was an Asian guy in back of the counter and no one else in the store.

A million thoughts raced through my head, none of them coherent. Only my stomach was making sense. It wanted me to just run in, grab some cold cuts and a loaf of bread, and get the hell out. I wouldn't even have to confront the guy. Let him decide if he was going to leave his store unattended and chase after me. Nope, that wasn't going to happen. I think I actually perked up a little, because all I could think about was being able to dump some food on the table when I got back home. But who was I kidding? It might be a nice fantasy, but it wasn't going to happen. I was too chicken shit.

The next thing I did was beyond stupid, and I still don't know what possessed me to head into the store and go straight up to the cash register. It was just like that day that my dad told me to get in there and beat up that neighborhood punk. I knew it was dumb. I knew I was probably going to get a beating, and I did it anyway. I watched myself doing something that made no sense at all and that was totally self-destructive, but that didn't stop me.

When I got to the cash register, I grabbed some gum, then asked the guy at the counter if I could use food stamps to buy more stuff. I probably had at least five dollars' worth on me. The way I remember it, he did not want to accept my food stamps, and man, we got into it. I was taller than him, and I think he immediately felt very threatened. Who could blame him? I wasn't a familiar face, and when he saw my anger over his rejecting the food stamps, he came at me with a tire iron. I looked around quickly for something to fend him off.

The only damn thing within reach was a stack of miniature pies on a rack, which I grabbed one by one and threw at him. I was trying to slow him down before he could whack me. Then I ducked forward to avoid one of his swings but that got me leaning over the counter. He reached and grabbed a handful of my T-shirt where it was tucked into the back of my jeans, so when I straightened out, the T-shirt came up over my head. Now I can't see shit and I'm real scared that I'm going to catch that tire iron in the face. So I spin a 180 and hightail it out of that store on a full sprint. When I got to my white Hyundai, I peeled the hell out of there. I thought it was a clean getaway too, because I didn't see nothing in my rearview. And I didn't see any bystanders that would be able to get my license plate number.

But I ended up being accused of robbery and assault. During a later trial that pitted me against the city of Los Angeles, the man from the store, Tae Suck Baik, testified that *I* had a tire iron inside my coat pocket that I took out when I had bought the pack of gum. He said I told him to open the cash register and that I took cash from it when he opened it. I allegedly also dove in to take some checks out of there, at which point Baik grabbed me by the arm. He said he told me I didn't need to take any checks. This is when the fight supposedly started. Baik said he was able to get hold of a metal rod and land several hits on me. I struck back. He says the tire iron I used allegedly came from my coat pocket, but I only recalled the pies on a nearby rack being the lone things I tossed at him, and I only threw them in self-defense.

My lawyer during the trial against L.A., Milton Grimes,

cross-examined Baik about the robbery. He questioned Baik's recollection that I told him to open the cash register, because Baik didn't speak English. And because he didn't speak English, how could he have understood and obeyed when I supposedly told him to open the cash register?

I had, and still have, no idea what Baik's level of English comprehension is, and I didn't stick around his store on the date of the incident to find out. Baik must've had the chance to catch a good view of my license plate and jot down the number, because the police came knocking ten days later and searched my car. In it, they discovered a check from Baik's grocery. The cops arrested me, and I decided not to put up a fight. I pleaded guilty to robbery.

It was a case of pies versus tire irons, and Baik's tire iron tale won. Now, granted, I didn't hit them with my pie story when the cops came around. I just plain said I was guilty. But I never really was. The only reason I pleaded guilty to the robbery charge is because I didn't have the money to hire a good lawyer.

I remember the lawyer I had was about four feet ten inches tall. He was extremely upset with me and kept asking me why I had said I was guilty. He told me to never talk to the cops and never admit anything. "You had this case beat," he claimed. "It was your word against his, and there was no one else around to witness it." Then he asked me what the hell I thought I was guilty of, what had I done wrong except to mess up a rack of pies? I just remember when I talked to those police, I was so embarrassed they had traced my license plate and were up in front of my home, I would have said anything to get them the hell out of there.

SENTENCED TO JAIL TERM

I was given a two-year sentence. That really upset me. In June, I wrote to the judge, asking him to cut down my time in prison. "Give me another chance, your honor," I said in my letter. "I have a good job and I have two fine boys (they were my second wife's children from another marriage) who wish me home. I have so much at stake to lose if I don't get that chance. My job and my family awaits me so please reconsider your judgment, your honor. The sky my witness and God knows."

Luckily, I was released on parole after one year.

The thing is, people who know me, know I'm not a violent guy—not the type of guy who'd stoop to robbery and assault. Anthony Beaty, who's a neighbor who has known me since I was a kid, said he was surprised by news of the robbery. "I didn't think he had that in him," he said. I admit I'm a big guy, but I don't like using my size to throw my weight around. I'm pretty quiet, for the most part. A friend even once described me as Baby Huey.

My parole agent, Tim Fowler, saw that mellow side in me. He thought I was guilty of the robbery, and I didn't blame him—because, after all, I did plead guilty—but when he speculated as to why I committed the "crime," he didn't say it was because I was a thug. He knew I was "unemployed and untrained" at the time of the alleged robbery, and he thought I was desperate because of that. He said, "It was something that wasn't planned, really. It was spur of the moment. The opportunity was there. He recognizes it was stupid." He didn't think of me as a hardened criminal. Even Baik didn't think I was a violent man. "He just wanted the money," Baik said about me. "I hit him first. If I didn't hit him, he wouldn't have hit me."

I think that's the thing that drives a lot of people crazy when they're looking for answers. They always want things to add up nice and neat and make sense. They always say, "If you did this, and then you said this, then why did this end up happening? What were you thinking? Didn't you realize that if you said this and then you did that, this would be the consequence?" The thing they'll never get is that a lot of times, even I can't explain why I did something, I really can't. I just got caught up in a very flawed way of thinking, and from that point on, it's almost like watching somebody else doing it.

That's exactly what happened the night I was beat up by those cops. I knew I should have just stopped driving the moment I saw those cruiser lights in my rearview mirror. And many people, to this day, ask me why I didn't just pull over when the police first started behind me on that fateful day. My answer is that I don't think I have an answer. I know a lot of explanations have been written down over the years, the most popular being that I was on parole and knew that I would get locked up as soon as I stopped so I was just trying to put off having to face the music. But I can't say for sure I actually thought it through like that when I was behind the wheel. I honestly believe I kept driving because I wasn't thinking, I was drinking, and there was hell to pay afterwards.

Like my mom used to say: "What did you do now?"

ONLY THE BEGINNING

So what went down at the convenience store in 1989, and the conviction that followed, turned out to be only the beginning of my troubles with the law. I started into the next decade like a boat without a rudder, bouncing around aimlessly, in and out of trouble with the law, going from a bad day to a good week to a bad month. One moment I'd be thrilled over having put in a solid week of work, cashing a healthy paycheck, and enjoying a well-fed, loving family, and the next I'd be totally out-of-control drinking, drugging, or driving, usually all three.

Although sentenced to two years behind bars after my 1989 conviction for the convenience store robbery in Monterey Park, I caught a first-time offender break when the sentence was reduced to one year. First-time offenders also got the option of working off some of the time in fire camp, which was the one of the coolest experiences I ever had in my life. We rode in helicopters, learned how to dig trenches in record time, and all sorts of cool maneuvers to shift, minimize, and extinguish forest fires. I learned how to fight forest fires the same time I was learning how to develop a little self-respect. And the truth is that I was very sad the day fire camp ended, because I loved working outdoors and was in great shape by the time I finished there.

Being in great shape, however, just attracted the wrong element where I was going next. I learned that being behind bars was like living on a different planet. There was an entirely different set of rules, and common sense and logic had nothing to do with it. There were times that I had to avoid being in a certain area of our dormlike quarters because it was being used for sex. I was only too happy to get out of there, and tried to stay invisible while serving out the rest of my sentence. The things they would do to some of the inmates were just beyond perverse. To make some of the inmates look more feminine, they would have their hair pulled back in ponytails and use the makeup they smuggled in to get them all dolled up. There seemed to be a limitless capacity for some inmates to have sex. It just freaked me out. The extent to which inmates would engage in sex with other inmates was all out of proportion with reality. I think it's very hard for anyone who has spent time in the joint to ever look again at sex as something sacred and beautiful. I don't care who they are or what they go back to—that perspective is lost forever. It is one of the great losses suffered after any significant time in prison, and it stays with you for life.

While behind bars, I would always look for something to lighten the burden—and I actually found something. For me, it was the fact that we had us a resident celebrity. It was none other than Ike Turner. Now, I only got to be near Ike a few times, but he had prison life licked. He had his own private cell, and nobody messed with him. Almost all prisoners shared a cell, but not with Ike, he had a cell all to himself. Ike also had a lifetime supply of chocolate, which he loved. I'm talking about stacks and stacks of almond and plain Hershey's bars. He had a couple of rats for pets that had crept into his cell from God knows where, and Ike used to feed them the chocolate, give them names, and pet them like a kid would hold a hamster. He was smart, though, because he kept the rest of the chocolate sealed tightly shut in cookie tins. Being around Ike was the one good memory I took with me after my year in the pen. He was the ultimate of cool. I remember him rocking out with his wife, Tina, in the early seventies, and I still smile when I think of him running the show in there.

THE BLACKEST NIGHT

I was still on parole for the convenience store incident when I got behind the wheel of my Hyundai on Friday, March 3, 1991, with my good friends Bryant "Pooh" Allen and Freddie Helms in the car. I was unemployed at the time but had just gotten a job and was to report to work that coming Monday. We had just watched a basketball game on TV, and it was still pretty early so we decided to go for a drive. Now, I'd been friends with these two guys for a while and even used to rap with Freddie, something I was doing more and more since I got out of jail. We had no definite destination in mind but talked about checking out a park where my father and I used hang out.

After ten, eleven P.M. in L.A., the highways are usually more open, and the flow of traffic easily gets into the high seventies to eighties. Trouble is, after a few miles at that speed, ninety starts to feel like eighty, and I must have been in the passing lane where cars can hit those speeds pretty easily. All of a sudden, a California Highway Patrol (CHP) officer, Melanie Singer, started chasing me because she said she clocked me going 115 mph on the Foothill Freeway and 80 mph on city streets. Singer wasn't the only one after me. The L.A. police were on my tail too. They chased me through city streets for 7.8 miles, where Singer reported I was topping speeds of 80 mph. The LAPD initially reported fifteen officers involved in the chase. Later reports say that there were twenty-one policemen on the scene, and twenty-seven officers total.

CHP and the LAPD claim they were chasing me because I was speeding, but recordings of CHP and LAPD talking on the radio at the time don't include anyone mentioning how fast I was going on the freeway. And here's the thing: the makers of my car, Hyundai, officially said that the car I was driving wasn't even capable of going faster than 100 mph. The tapes did say, though, that I was clocked at 65 mph on city streets, and that seems closer to the truth.

THE BEATING

This section is going to get pretty ugly, but it is the God's honest truth and has to be written down so it can be understood what happened to me that night. The chase finally ended about fifteen minutes later at Lake View Terrace when I came face-to-face with a pickup truck and couldn't drive anymore. Timothy Singer, Melanie Singer's CHP partner, who was also her husband, approached my car. He talked to me, and Pooh and Freddie and I got out of the car.

Lawyers for the police later said the cops thought I was dangerous. Tests showed that my blood alcohol level was two times past the state's legal limit when they stopped me, but I was definitely not on PCP, as the officers claimed. There were tests done to check on the PCP, and they back me up on this. There were no traces of the drug in me.

But the cops were convinced I was high on alcohol and psychedelics, and they said I resisted arrest. That is not true, but they used it as their reason to use force. The initial LAPD reports say the cops had to hit me with a baton several times and shoot me twice with a Taser gun because I supposedly attacked them.

In court, Melanie Singer testified that instead of seeing me act aggressively, she saw me smile. She said I was "jovial" and that I even waved to the helicopter that the police had sent to hover above me. She also said I pointed my right butt cheek at her and wiggled it and that I went down and acted "like a dog" walking on all fours. If what she said is true, then it was silly behavior on my part, but I don't think it could be viewed as dangerous to the cops surrounding me. I point this out in a later chapter, but when officers can't see your hands, they get real nervous and assume the worst. That's what happened when they initially had me up against the car to frisk me for any weapons or drugs I may have had hidden in my pockets, underwear, shirt, socks, or shoes. For one blessed second, the angle of my body obscured the officers' sight line of my left hand, and that made them extremely suspicious and nervous.

The female officer moved in to arrest me. Melanie Singer testified that she approached me with her gun pointed at me. I lay down on the ground as she commanded, and everything was cool. She had taken my ID and was just getting ready to slap the handcuffs on me. She said she was about five feet away from me when Sergeant Stacey C. Koon told her to stop and back away. Singer said the cops pounced on me, all of them trying to cuff me.

But that was not their intent, and that was made brutally clear to me when one of the officers suddenly kicked me with his boot in the side of my face, smashing my jaw! It felt like someone had taken a baseball bat to my head. Before I could even register that unbearable pain, one of the other officers slammed me in the lower leg with his baton. I heard a crack and was so damn surprised when that happened that I immediately pleaded with Melanie. I know this is going to sound kind of strange, but up until that point, I had felt safe with her there at the scene, sort of a maternal presence that would not allow things to get too out of control. I shouted out to her, "They don't have to do this! Tell them they don't have to do this!" Melanie actually responded, but it sent me into the worst panic because it was just a barely audible "huh," and that's when the fear flooded into me. But then the officer who had kicked me bent down over me and said, "How do you feel?" Just like that the fear was gone, replaced by some jock attitude that wasn't going to let this son of a bitch get the better of me. I tried to respond but had to spit out a mouthful of blood before I could speak. Then I said it, "I feel fine."

I was sure that the police thought me spitting out that ball of blood was meant as a defiant gesture, and I pulled back at that point. Suddenly I was thinking through this mother-fucking situation, telling myself, "Now Glen, do not make any sudden moves or you are sure as hell going to catch a bullet." (Glen is my middle name, and it's always been the name my family and others close to me have preferred using.) I could smell the hatred, it was a clear presence. Me saying that I felt fine set something off in them police, and although it gave me the briefest of satisfaction, I knew I could not do anything that could even remotely be viewed as aggressive or they would shoot my ass dead.

Suddenly I was being hit with multiple baton blows to every part of my body—my knees, ankles, wrists, and head. The beatings continued to rain down on me. Singer called them power strokes. When she was in court, Deputy District Attorney Terry White asked her to show the power stroke, and when she did you could tell people were shocked. They gasped in the courtroom when they saw how strong the blow was. It's like swinging a baseball bat at full speed, trying to hit it with all your strength. There's also some kind of diamond-shaped groove in the baton that leaves a horrible cut in the skin.

The repeated smashing of my body gave me the strongest urge to piss my pants, but I would not let them do that to me. Instead, I instinctually started trying to cover up my nuts with one hand and the back of my head with the other. This only made them more furious, and they started yelling the craziest shit at me. I stopped thinking and tried to get up and run. But my damn leg wasn't working right, and that's when I realized my ankle was broken. That busted joint probably saved my life, because I could not run in *any* direction without it looking like I was running at a cop. And if there was a time, that night, that I was going to give them an excuse to kill me, that was it. I threw my hands up to show them I was surrendering, and lay back down as fast as I could. Although that got me scared again because it made me realize my body wasn't working right at all. If it wasn't listening to what I wanted it to do, I must have been hurt bad.

Now this was about the time that George Holliday began to videotape the beating. He got me at the beginning of me trying to escape, and then got most of the beating and kicking by the cops. Holliday, who lived in an apartment building nearby, was woken up by all the sirens and loud voices. He grabbed his new video camera and stepped out onto his balcony. There was a helicopter hovering overhead. And he saw me, on the ground screaming, the cops circled me. If you watch the eighty-one-second video, you'll see that the cops came at me with their batons and hit me more than fifty times.

I know this: it infuriated the officers to see that I hadn't taken the bait, that I had gotten right back down, but no credit to me there. I was just fortunate to have my ankle broken so badly that I couldn't run on it even if I tried. The pain was unbelievable, but I just looked down at my flopped over leg and knew I was spending the rest of that night lying down. The baton smashes continued, but now they were in clumps, as if one cop would batter the shit out of my face, neck, arms, and legs until he got tired, and then another officer would take over. I kept reminding myself to stay cool, but it was as if I was some damn human piñata and the cops were all in a rush to see who could smash me open first.

Then I got very upset because the damn cops had made me piss in my pants after all. I had the craziest thought at that moment, I began to think about all the blacks down South who were slaves and had been beaten and lynched. I felt a strange power at that moment, as if their spirits were all coming together to help me through this. And the first thing I did was to apologize to them for being weak and pissing myself! But when I pulled my hand away from my nuts I could see that they weren't wet from any urine—they were soaked in my blood. That's why my pants felt all wet and heavy. I was bleeding everywhere, just leaking out my life there on the asphalt. I got scared again, because the cops kept yelling for me to get up again and run because they were definitely going to kill me. Why didn't you keep running the first time? Didn't I realize that this was it for me?

At first every baton blow was a terrible shock of the most horrible pain, kind of like Daddy being at his drunkest extension-cord-swinging worst, but after about twenty of those baton hits, I got real scared because although I could clearly hear my bones cracking, the searing pain was starting to become duller.

That's when I told myself, "Glen, you got to live through this. Them slaves had it no better than this, and you must not let them down. Do not let them down. Make them proud of what you can take. You can take anything they can dish out. No matter what they do to you, you've got to keep breathing, you've got to stay alive! You have got to stay alive! . . . and that's when I felt somebody's boot slam my face into the street real hard. It definitely surprised the hell out of me, but then, oh my dear God, my whole body just shook violently in a horrible spasm. It took me a few seconds to figure out that Officer Koon had just sent 50,000 volts through my body with a Taser shock.

I thought I knew every kind of pain possible, but that was just terrible. I realized the cop wasn't worried about getting shocked because the soles of those boots must be made out of some kind of rubber. The horrible fact was that the blood soaking through all my clothes made the electrocution worse because my body was all wet! Only one thing could make this situation worse: shocking me again—because my body, my heart, was still trying to cling to life. Then Koon zapped me with the Taser again. That's when all my reasoning collapsed in on me, and I realized I was going to die. I started to think about all the bad things I had done in my life, and that at least the Lord might see this beating as some kind of penance for the sins I had committed. I don't remember actually praying to God that night, but I do recall thinking about the Almighty, and that maybe all this pain would be over soon. But then another baton blow came down, one of the last, to fracture my eye socket, and I despaired of just about everything. I had let down my slave ancestors, I had been a sinner, and now I was going to die. A horrible spasm of pain shook my entire body and I realized the cops were hog tying me up.

My last thoughts were pretty pathetic: I was worried because there was so much blood in my mouth, and I didn't want to spit and hit any of the cops. They might hit me again. Please just don't—and then I gave it up to the blackest night and mercifully passed out for a while.

I was put away in the Los Angeles County Jail after this run-in with the cops. I spent three days there before they released me. No charges were filed against me, even though the cops said they chased me because I was speeding.

I'm not one for publicity, but I did make a public appearance to talk about what happened. I told people, "I was scared for my life" when the cops came after me with their weapons. "So I laid down real calmly and took it like a man."

But I didn't feel like a man that night, even though I had survived. I felt like a child, helpless. I remember that night, after the beating, when I was at the hospital, my mom walked right by me. My face was so messed up, my own mother didn't even recognize her son. I didn't notice she was there because I was too busy trying to find a bag to put my jeans in. They was soaked clear through with blood, and the doctors had to cut them off me. I stopped one of the nurses from throwing them away. She got kind of annoyed when I asked her to hand them back. I told her I needed them for evidence because I was afraid no one would believe what happened to me. I had my Vans in my other hand. They were all tore up and drenched in blood too.

I was holding on to everything tight. The pain was beyond intense. It kept coming in waves, but for some reason I couldn't just pass out again. I wish I had, because my mom let out an awful sound when they told her that lump of raw ground chuck on the table was me. I didn't want her to see me that way. I was afraid she'd say, "What did you do now? What could you possibly do to deserve this?"

I was in such bad shape that Pacifica Hospital recommended I be sent to L.A. County Medical Center where they could fix me up. What was nuts was that between hospitals, they actually stopped off at the Foothill Station. I think they wanted to show me off. It was surreal, and I remember being in the backseat with my body cramping and bleeding, and just trying to hang on. But by that point, I was certain I was going to be disfigured and handicapped for life, and that put me in the worst state of depression.

Later, after they moved me to a second hospital to get the proper medical attention, I was still determined to hang on to my shoes. The torn skin on my hands was sticking to the canvas on my Vans, and it hurt like hell when I eventually tried to set them down. Everything on me was getting stiff and cold. It was like parts of me were tired of bleeding and just wanted to give up. I started to feel like a dead person. "What's the use?" I was thinking. "I am busted up beyond broken—no way they'll be able to fix me up. And no goddamn way they'll ever believe what happened."

It was time to check out. Join my brothers in the hereafter. I didn't care, I just wanted to die. Float up and move on, because only the unbearable pain was keeping me alive, and who wanted that? Then I heard a voice, and it sounded like it belonged to an angel. I looked up to see it was an older, black female cop. She told me I didn't have to worry about hanging on to no pants or shoes. She said that someone had a tape of the whole thing, and they were going to see what happened and believe everything I said.

At first, I didn't understand what she was saying. She just calmly repeated what she said, that I didn't have to worry, that they were going to believe everything I told them because there was proof. And I *still* didn't get what she was saying. What kind of proof? It was dark, and I didn't see anybody around except them cops.

When it finally sunk in, I just cried. It was wonderful and it was horrible, and I kept thanking the good Lord that he hadn't walked away from me, even though I knew I had done wrong and I was a sinner. It was the first time anything had gone my way in a long, long time.

THE TRIAL

On March 4, ten days after the video tape showing Rodney's beating first aired on KTLA and then was shown all over the country, an L.A. County grand jury weighed in on what happened that night and indicted Police Officers Koon, Laurence M. Powell, Theodore J. Briseno, and Timothy E. Wind for felony assault. They all pleaded not guilty on March 26. Wind was a rookie cop, and the LAPD dismissed him after the beating, while the other three officers only got a suspension without pay.

Bernard Kamins was the original judge to preside over the trial of the officers. A change of venue for the trial was granted, though, with a new judge, Stanley M. Weisberg, presiding. Judge Weisberg decided to re-set the trial in Ventura County. Opening arguments took place on March 4, 1992, in front of a jury that looked a bit funny for a case like this. There were ten white jurors, one Asian, and one Hispanic. I go into this more in a later chapter, when I focus more on the courtroom drama. This is just a bare-bones account.

Melanie Singer testified that even though I was on my knees and not resisting arrest, Powell hit my head and face with six blows of his metal baton. He did this while I was still in a highly disoriented state as a result of Koon's Taser shots. Even though I was Tasered, I wasn't knocked down, and the cops later testified that they thought I was on PCP because I was able to remain standing. But the LAPD did acknowledge that medical tests proved I had no traces of PCP in me.

Singer said that when Koon saw Powell hitting me, he told him, "Stop! Stop! That's enough!" She also said that Briseno tried to stop Powell from hitting me by pushing Powell's baton away from me. Michael Stone, Powell's lawyer, said Powell wasn't the cause of my face being busted up. He said the mess happened when I hit the pavement, not when Powell's baton hit me and kept on hitting me.

Come trial time, the cops fought against one another. Koon and Briseno tried to pit themselves against the other two officers to make it seem like the others were the ones who had used excessive force. John Barnett, Briseno's lawyer, singled out Powell and Wind and said they were "out of control" in using their weapons on me. In the video of the beating, it looks like Briseno kicked me, because he did. But Barnett tried to manipulate this interpretation by saying it actually looked like Briseno had been protecting me from being beaten by Powell and Wind by keeping me down with his foot. Unbelievable.

I don't know much about the officers' professional behavior, except for what happened during the beating, but here's what's on the record and what I recollect about them at the time of the trial. Koon, the one who Tasered me, testified that he was the cop in charge during the incident. He said that what happened was a "managed and controlled use of force" and that he was following the "policies of the Los Angeles Police Department and the training." He said he tried to stop the blows coming down on me. His report on the incident said I only wound up with "minor" injuries, but there's a computer that cops evidently use to send messages back and forth to each other as a way of touting their actions. Koon called the whole thing "a big time use of force." The charges on Koon included assault with a deadly weapon, use of excessive force under color of authority, falsification of a police report, and accessory after the fact. He would've gotten a max of seven years and eight months if convicted.

In the video, Powell is shown hitting me over and over with his baton and kicking me. You can see him hitting my head more than five times. He testified that he did all this because "I was completely in fear for my life, scared to death." After the beating, he went back to his cop car and sent a computer message that said, "I haven't beaten anyone this bad in a long time." But the report he wrote up about it said I had only "contusions and abrasions" as a result of what happened. What I really had was a lot of broken bones.

Now, I don't know if Powell is a racist, but evidence submitted in court shows that twenty minutes before he beat me, he sent this computer message: "Sounds almost exciting as our last call. It was right out of *Gorillas in the Mist*." Powell's lawyer tried to dismiss this comment about his interpretation of activities at a black household by saying it wasn't necessarily racist, but Deputy D.A. Terry White said that Powell's message "shows motive and also bias by Mr. Powell against Rodney King because he is black."

I'm not the first one that Powell beat up either. He got in trouble earlier in his career because he hit a man named Salvador Castaneda with his baton. He got in one to five blows and broke the man's elbow. Powell said Castaneda came towards him to attack, but Castaneda said he wasn't being aggressive. He said he didn't resist Powell. Powell got hit with a lawsuit charging him with use of excessive force. It was settled out of court. Castaneda got $70,000 for his troubles. In my case, the charges on Powell included assault with a deadly weapon, use of excessive force under color of authority, and falsification of a police report. He would've received the same maximum sentence that Koon would have if convicted.

Wind was a rookie police officer. Powell was his supervisor the night of the beating, and when Powell started hitting me,

Wind allegedly followed his lead and beat me with his baton and kicked me. You can see him in action on the video. The charges on Wind included assault with a deadly weapon and use of excessive force under color of authority. He would've gotten a maximum sentence of seven years if he had been convicted. Wind never testified at the trial.

Briseno can be seen in the video kicking me once. During the trial, he tried to make it seem he wasn't like the other three cops the night of the beating. He said outright that he blamed the others for what happened, saying that I was already laying down and that Powell kept hitting me while Koon didn't do anything to stop him. He singled out Koon for possibly starting the beating. He testified, "I just thought the whole thing was out of control."

Back in 1987, Briseno was suspended for hitting and kicking a suspect that was already handcuffed. He admitted then that he had been "a little too aggressive." He also said he wouldn't let it happen again. The charges on Briseno in my case included assault with a deadly weapon and use of excessive force under color of authority. He would've gotten a maximum sentence of four years if convicted.

Deputy D.A. White kept showing the video of the beating to the jury to make his case against the officers. His plan was to call me to the stand, but in the end, he decided not to. He chose not to call me up to testify because my memories of what happened that night weren't so clear. He was afraid that I might have said something that wouldn't sit right with what other witnesses said. He thought that because of the multiple skull fractures, I might not have had sharp recall and might even have said something that would go against evidence in the videotape.

On April 23, 1992, the case went to the jury for them to decide the fate of the officers. They came back six days later on April 29 and pronounced a verdict of not guilty for all four cops. The only thing they couldn't agree on was the charge on Powell for use of excessive force. They were a hung jury on that one. The jurors were mostly white and so were the cops, except Briseno was part Hispanic. I go into my personal feelings about this in a later chapter.

Ted Koppel from the show *Nightline* sat down with one of the jurors, who didn't want people to know his identity. This juror explained that even though the video of me getting beat up was shown over and over in court, the fact that I didn't get up on the stand and speak out against the cops made the jury think that the video was weak evidence. The juror also complained the video was shaky and blurry. "The cops were simply doing what they'd been instructed to do. . . . They were afraid he was going to run or even attack them," the juror said. The juror didn't think my injuries were serious, either. "A lot of those blows, when you watched them in slow motion, were not connecting. . . . Those batons are heavy, but when you looked at King's body three days after the incident, not that much damage was done."

Tom Bradley, who was mayor back then and used to be a police officer, thought differently. "The jury's verdict will never blind us to what we saw on that videotape. The men who beat Rodney King do not deserve to wear the uniform of the LAPD," he said.

Bill Clinton, who was governor of Arkansas at the time, said, "Like most of America I saw the tape of the beatings several times, and it certainly looks excessive to me so I don't understand the verdict."

Chapter 3

THE BURNING OF LOS ANGELES

THE RIOTS

The day the L.A. riots erupted in the streets of South Central, it was like the entire city had finally caught up with what had been simmering inside me for months. From the information Tom Owens was relaying to me over the phone, the trial wasn't going well for us. Owens was an investigator hired to assist with the case by my attorney Steven Lerman. He gave me information after talking with Steve in the bathroom of the courthouse during recesses. Tom was a bright guy and I was glad to have him on our team. He used to check under each bathroom stall before speaking with Lerman. I began to sense that Officers Powell, Koon, Wind, and Briseno were going to walk. Evidently a lot of other people shared the same feeling because word on the street, as early as three days before the verdict, was that if these guys walked, a full-scale riot was inevitable.

It was Owens who called me with the devastating news about the acquittal of all four officers. I had been forced to sit in my home, like a caged animal against its will, while the entire trial played out. I was inwardly furious that they had never even considered putting me up there on the stand. Those jurors needed to see the person, look into the eyes and hear the voice of the victim in that video. By the time every news outlet in the United States announced the acquittal, my shock and rage was so overwhelming that I just wanted to close my eyes and open them as another person someplace a thousand miles away. It felt like the trial had been stacked against me from the start, like there was a manipulation happening in that courtroom. And it was powerful. It sounded like the jurors would view something with their own eyes, but were told by the lawyers to give it a different interpretation. Sure the Taser delivered 50,000 volts into my body, but look! King is still moving after the first shock, he's still conscious after the second, so Officer Koon couldn't have hurt him that badly. It was nothing short of brainwashing, as if the defense attorneys were saying over and over again, "What you see is not what happened. You've grown up knowing that color is blue, but for this trial, we're going to say it's red, and that's what you must agree to believe."

I couldn't stop thinking about what Mayor Bradley had said the year before, right after the tape went public: he said the men who beat me did not deserve to wear the uniform of the Los Angeles Police. I had held on to that statement over the year, just as much as I'd held on to what President Bush had said, a couple weeks after the beating: "It was sickening to see the beating that was rendered and there's no way, no way in my view, to explain that away." These statements had kept my hopes alive, that justice would prevail. But the cops' lawyers had managed to explain it away. Somehow, they made the jurors believe I was the dangerous presence that night and the police were justified in doing what they did to me.

SUMMATION

The jurors had actually held a standard issue LAPD steel baton in their hands—just like the one that had been used by Powell, Wind, and Briseno—and they knew how hard and heavy it was. But they were told that the blows must not have been that bad. They watched the video again and again of Koon sending 50,000 volts into me, but were told that because I got back up, it wasn't so gruesome. I told Lerman that I challenged anyone to lie perfectly still after being Tasered. It is a physical impossibility. But their team repeatedly told the jury that my injuries weren't that serious, and that I was a tall, muscular, imposing man that scared the police and had to be taken down. At some point, this reasoning all sank in, and I was sunk.

The incredible feeling of redemption I experienced when I was told by a black policewoman that someone had videotaped my beating was gone. The George Holliday videotape seemed to have no impact on the jury. Perhaps it was because after they had seen it so many times, the video just lost its effect. The first night that the jury went into deliberation, I sat with my mom in front of the TV. She didn't say a thing. But at one point she squeezed my hand at something the news anchorman said, and that's when I knew she knew. She may as well have just said it. "Justice is not in the cards for you, Glen."

I don't remember all my feelings precisely, but I was probably in a kind of shock about the whole thing. I know I was content to stay in the house until the family started coming around that evening. We were going to just sit and eat and talk, like we had done as a family countless times before, anything to get my mind off what had happened that day. But that evening of BBQ and beers didn't end up the way I thought it would.

We were all sitting in the backyard of my place in Studio City—Momma, my brothers, my younger sister, and a couple of friends had gathered simply to show their support and love for me. I was talking mainly about my great love, baseball. Baseball season had just started and it was that magical time when every team was in it, just starting to compete, and anything was possible. I used to play third base, outfield, and even shortstop once in a while. Baseball is the greatest sport on earth, and I was blabbing on and on, just thrilled to be talking about anything but that trial. It was great not having anyone calling the house and ordering us around, telling us when to be ready, what to wear, and where we had to be the next day. My brothers lit a few tiki torches, and we just took in the night. It was almost May, and we could feel a nice spring breeze blowing through the valley.

The trial was over, over, over. It affected different people in different ways, and I can remember thinking some Angelenos just went kind of crazy. But at that moment, I wasn't thinking about the initial shouting on the courtroom steps, or their looks of disbelief. I was mainly upset about the way all them police got off, and was trying to get my mind to a better place. That night, Momma, in her wisdom and healing way, was already moving on. She encouraged me to do the same, and insisted I try my best to drop it. "Time to let it all go," she kept saying. "Just let it go, Glen." She felt the sooner I got it behind me, the sooner I could go back to a normal life. The last year had sure been rough on her. On all of us.

So we were sitting on this busted-up lawn furniture. Momma could see that I was starting to get emotional about the whole ordeal again and was just starting to say something when one of my brothers blurted, "Hey! Over there!" We looked up to catch the tail end of what looked like a signal flair you might see the military use. Someone had shot it off over what looked to be South Central, and it was just dying out as we turned to watch it.

Unlike most people, who learned about it on TV or on the radio while driving, that's the way my family and I witnessed the beginning of the Los Angeles riots, although we did not know that at the time.

Eventually when we were back inside watching TV, we found out that the riots had started almost instantly. We learned that when the verdicts were read aloud in the courtroom mid-afternoon Wednesday, reactions began almost simultaneously in various parts of Los Angeles, about an hour southeast of the Simi Valley courthouse where I had sat shocked and motionless.

"We want justice!" and "Honk your horns for guilty!" chanted a crowd of two hundred or so that gathered at Lake View Terrace—where the beating had been videotaped by George Holliday more than a year before. They carried makeshift signs with "No Justice for a Brother" scrawled in block letters. A few rocks pelted passing police cars, but the mostly black crowd pretty much stuck to using chants and signs to show their anger and disappointment.

Across town at police headquarters, a few hundred demonstrators demanded that Chief of Police Gates resign. It didn't take long for them to get so worked up they stormed the building. They actually tried to force their way into police headquarters! That level of rage should have been a sign of things to come. The police were able to hold off the crowd there, of course, but as the afternoon wore on, it was clear they weren't prepared for what was already in motion.

Within a couple hours, a bunch of activist organizations added their outcries over the verdicts. The National Association for the Advancement of Colored People, the American Civil Liberties Union, the American Jewish Congress, the Los Angeles Gay and Lesbian Community Services Center, and the Gay & Lesbian Alliance Against Defamation/Los Angeles all weighed in. Many leaders condemned the verdict as a travesty of justice.

IMAGES OF DOOM

Shocking images started flashing on the television. One of the first ones I saw was of the four police officers who had been accused. The media cameras caught them congratulating each other and hugging their attorneys, smiling like it was Christmas. Those images made my head ache and my heart hurt, but I had no clue over the extent of what was to follow.

Arsonists set the first fires before nightfall. And only an hour after the verdict, the first store got busted up by some kids angry about the verdict. They said cameras captured the shattered storefront sixty-two minutes after the gavel came down. I guessed that was as long as anybody could hold their anger in. By early evening, it was becoming very clear that the urgent calls for calm and peace by the mayor and civic leaders were falling on deaf ears. Fears of violence and destruction began to become a reality. In many of the neighborhoods in South Central, you could hear yelling and shouting that sounded half angry, half joyful. On television you could see people waving to the media and laughing as plate glass windows shattered and boutiques, drug stores, delis, and shops went up in flames.

Over the years I heard a lot from eyewitnesses about what happened that first night. As soon as people began to set fires and smash stuff, a gang of professional criminals went downtown and took advantage of the confusion and chaos. With chains, winches, and heavy-duty pickups, they ripped ATMs right out of their moorings and dragged them away to special chop shops where they could cut them open. They were all in and out in less than an hour. Real pros. Them white collars got the first haul.

VINDICATION

Now, I am not ashamed to admit that for the first few hours, before I heard about anyone getting killed or even hurt yet, I felt a certain vindication. I believed I was witnessing the simple fact that other people were mad as hell about the verdict.

But it wasn't long before the fury exploded, and whatever vindication I felt became a terrible sense of guilt and sadness— and this all happened in the blink of an eye.

If there is a ground zero for the L.A. riots, it would have to be this little patch of South Central L.A., a two-and-a-half-square-mile box. It's packed there, one of the city's most crowded neighborhoods, crammed in between I-10 and I-110. If you don't know Los Angeles, it's hard to explain how different it is from the pictures you see on television and in movies. No pretty palm trees and manicured lawns or any of that. No fancy boutiques or pretty buildings with shiny windows. All the big houses of Beverly Hills may only be about ten miles to the north, and the beautiful beach houses on the ocean in Malibu only about ten miles to the west, but those places might as well be a million miles away.

Right smack in the middle of that area, at the intersection of Florence and Normandie Avenues, two horrific beatings took place that got broadcast on live network TV and beamed right into my living room only a few hours after the verdict. Both of them broke my heart and made me feel like the world I'd been a part of for twenty-seven years had cracked so badly, it might never be fixed. They were like anti-Kodak moments of the riots, and they got played over and over again just like the tape of my beating had been. It was the saddest thing: a year after everybody, all over the world, had watched me get beaten, we were all sitting in front of our televisions watching other people getting beaten. It destroyed me. I felt like we weren't in America, like the city I loved had been turned into some kind of war zone, and it was only going to get worse.

TRIBUTE?

Suddenly, I heard a couple of trucks pull up outside my home. My family all walked outside to see who was joining us. It was one of my cousins by marriage. He popped out of his cab and happily threw his arms around me. I noticed that the bed of his truck was filled with all kinds of stuff—from liquor to food to disposable diapers.

"Here you go, man," he said, smiling.

"What do you mean?" I asked him.

"Payback, Homes. Payback. You deserve this shit. It's the least you should be getting."

I got the chills all over when he said that, because I was touched by his words. But I was also kinda scared for some reason. I looked in one of the cases of booze and I could see that a few of the bottleneck labels of Jack Daniels were charred from a fire, but the liquor was in fine shape, and I was really tempted. Man, was I tempted.

"Take it, Glen!" he said loudly. "Take it! Or at least let me dump it off here, because there's lots more where that came from." He was amped, ready to do another run. There were two other guys with him, and they were saying, "C'mon, we got to go. We got to go now!"

While I was trying to decide whether to take the stuff, a few more friends rolled up in SUVs and hatchbacks, all filled to the brim with tons of goods. Each had the same idea: they were bringing all kinds of stuff for me and my family. They could have taken off for their homes and stashed all of it for themselves, but they wanted me to have first dibs. Said it was the right thing to do. I got the chills again, getting very emotional and almost crying right there as I stood on the sidewalk.

Situations like that, when the excitement is overwhelming but the fear is clutching my chest, I can never make up my mind. I remember that my girlfriend at the time had a baby, and she was tugging on my shirt, bugging me: "At least grab the Pampers. That shit's expensive." I didn't spend much time with the merchandise, though. I just thanked everybody and waved them on, watched them cruise on down the street. There was so much stuff that the rear axles were almost dragging on the ground. But this was all just a temporary distraction. I was way more concerned with what was going on downtown.

I was so curious, I went up to the attic and grabbed an old

Bob Marley wig we used to keep around for Halloween. You could never tell it was me with all them dreadlocks hanging down. Well, I put that sucker on and drove down near the action just to see what the hell was happening. Within a couple blocks of Normandie, I had to stop. I sensed that terrible presence of hatred that I felt the night of the beating, that palpable wall of loathing that was absolutely suffocating. I mean there were sounds like I never heard before, like evil erupting. I lowered the window and heard what I thought was a high-tension wire that had snapped off from its tower and was spraying sparks all over the place. But it could have been a blown transformer, I really had no idea.

There were hoots and screams and lots of urgent loud yelling. It was both terrifying and seductive. I wanted to get closer, God I wanted to look right into the face of it all, but then I heard gunshots going off—they always sound like cheap fireworks. That's when I turned around and headed the fuck out of there. The voice that had ordered me to stay alive the night of the beating was back, commanding me to get on home. There was no sense in me catching a stray slug after what I had been through.

REGINALD DENNY

Any conflicted feelings about what was going on were totally crushed when I got home and saw what happened to Reginald Denny. I'll never forget the first time I saw the video footage of

Denny. He was a white truck driver, thirty-six, who was just an average guy who made the near-fatal decision to stop at a traffic light and was dragged out of the truck and beaten to a pulp by a mob of local black residents. News helicopters hovered above, recording every blow. A concrete fragment slammed into Denny's temple, and a cinder block landed on his head. He was completely helpless, lying unconscious in the street. There were no police present to help Denny, because they were ordered to withdraw in the early stages of the riots for their own safety.

An unarmed African-American civilian and true hero, Bobby Green Jr., rescued Reginald Denny. Green's courage and determination were inspiring. He had actually seen the assault live on TV from his home a few blocks away from the actual incident and rushed to the scene. He drove Denny to the hospital in Denny's eighteen-wheeler truck, which was hauling twenty-seven tons of sand.

When I saw the side of Denny's truck, something started to pick at me, and continued to haunt me until I realized something that brought this whole horrible incident a lot closer to me. I had worked construction on and off over the years and I knew the supply company Denny worked for. My boss did business with some of their truckers because we used their sand for cement mixing. It was highly likely that I mixed cement from a load of sand Reginald Denny brought us. Having that awareness stuck in my head tore me up awful inside.

FIDEL LOPEZ

Shortly after Denny was rescued, another beating was caught on camera—right around the corner from that intersection. Fidel Lopez, also a construction worker, was ripped from his truck and robbed of a couple grand. As one attacker smashed his forehead open with a car stereo, another rioter tried to slice his ear off. After Lopez lost consciousness, the crowd spray painted his torso and genitals black.

An African-American minister, the Rev. Bennie Newton, who ran an inner-city ministry for troubled youth, came to Lopez's aid by preventing others from further beating Lopez. He wedged himself between Lopez and his attackers, and shouted at the mob, "Kill him and you have to kill me too."

Rev. Bennie Newton and Bobby Green Jr. were incredibly courageous men. What they did was true heroism.

BLAME IT ON ME

Although network footage showed some pockets of unruly activity, the initial riot activity seemed almost like playful mischief. With children gathering along the streets to watch the insanity, the entire riot quickly became pure evil. It was as if the devil had decided to take over. Although I had heard chants of "No justice, no peace!", this looked like something no peaceful person could ever be a part of. As people of different ethnicities clashed, the riots became the heart of darkness.

Once I saw this series on the National Geographic Channel about evolution. That first night people devolved, I could see the primitive beast back in them.

I got that tight feeling in my chest and was suddenly seized by a terrible sense of responsibility as I heard the reports that started coming in about people being injured and killed. It was a living, breathing nightmare to me, with horrifying images pouring out of the TV like Armageddon.

Momma and my sister were scared worst of all. They were convinced the police were going to find some way to blame it all on me. Toss me in jail and throw away the key. My sister was crying, saying they'd probably ask for the death penalty. That had me completely terrified all night, just waiting for sirens outside my house.

My family sat with me in front of the TV that continued showing all the shocking news. It was impossible to take it all in and just as difficult to look away. I kept thinking about victims Denny and Lopez, because I knew how it felt to be beaten to death's door. The pain, the confusion, the helplessness. I knew the taste of the asphalt and the gagging blood. I knew what it felt like to reach out for help, to beg for it to stop, but it just kept going.

I remembered wondering that very night if Denny would see justice done before I did. It's been a long time since then for Denny, just as it's been a long time since then for me. I was happy to find out that with years of physical therapy Denny has recovered much of his basic skills. Part of that journey was to learn how to move past all that pain to forgiveness. If he's like me, he has to find a way to forgive every day.

By the time I tried to go to sleep the first night, four people had died and dozens were in the hospital. Hundreds more were in area hospitals with gunshot wounds. Soon the number would be ten times that. It's what violence always does—it just creates more violence.

As I lay in bed trying to sleep, the government was getting nervous. Governor Pete Wilson ordered the National Guard to report for duty. But they couldn't. They didn't have riot gear or enough ammunition, so they refused to come to South Central. The city, the state, even the National Guard—nobody had any idea that something of this magnitude was coming. The racial tensions that had been brewing in Los Angeles for the past year had been ignored.

Mayor Tom Bradley did his best. He got on television at eleven P.M. and pledged that the city would "take whatever resources needed" to stop the violence. He confirmed that calls for assistance had been sent to the county sheriff's department, the California Highway Patrol, and police and fire departments from neighboring cities. But no matter what the mayor was doing, it wasn't enough.

"We believe that the situation is now simmering down, pretty much under control," he said. The fact was that the violence was just beginning. Momma said it felt just like it did twenty-seven years before when the Watts riots raged. That was 1965, the year I was born. I'd gone by 103rd Street in Watts a hundred times. Back in '65, it had been completely burned to the ground. Folks started calling it Charcoal Alley. Momma remembered those riots—I was only a few months old. And now she was frightened, worse than ever. I felt so helpless as the events of the last year began to play themselves out in my mind. From the night of the beating when it all began until now, it was just one long sad tale of me never having control over anything in my life.

To be fair to Mayor Bradley, what was happening on the streets of L.A. was beyond anybody's control. Many of the city's most prominent and ethnically diverse organizations, like Urban League and the National Association for the Advancement of Colored People, called emergency meetings to put out a unified message of hope and restraint. Despite their repeated pleas, it appeared that their statements went unheard in the streets. President Bush issued a statement from the White House, condemning the violence and pleading for calm. Asked whether he supported the verdicts, the president hedged, saying that he was completely focused on quelling the violence at hand. Bill Clinton, the Arkansas governor who was emerging at the time to be Bush's likely opponent, spoke out against the violence from Birmingham, where he was campaigning.

But nothing helped.

SHUTTING DOWN

The riots didn't slow come the first morning. By the time I woke up, the city I'd spent almost my entire life in was literally in flames. Reports of fires were coming in at a rate of about one per minute. A normal night might bring two fires per hour citywide. By dawn, more than 150 fires raged in the city. And firefighters couldn't even get to the buildings that were ablaze. All the debris in the street from wrecked cars, and the sporadic but continuing gunfire kept the LAFD from getting where they needed to go. It was nothing short of chaos, and you could feel it in the air.

I left my house to take a walk around, and I could smell smoke the moment I stepped outside. By the time I reached the street, I could see towers of black smoke—dozens of them—rising from the city. It looked like Los Angeles had just gotten bombed. On the news, one city councilman compared the growing violence to conditions occurring "in Third World societies in the midst of collapsing juntas." It may have been the same councilman, but I'm not sure, who said that it set back race relations in L.A. more than two decades.

I was going to run to the store for some badly needed items, but I heard none of them were open. Everybody was so afraid, they were closing their shops and businesses even if they weren't near the center of the riots. They figured the riots would just continue to spread—and fast. It was like the city was getting ready for a hurricane. Everybody was trying to get more supplies for their homes, but shop owners continued boarding up their stores. As I stood watching the smoke rise, I thought this is what Armageddon will feel like.

Bus service was canceled. Electrical power outages were occurring all over the city. People who were on the job were sent home early, and everybody was ordered to stay in their homes. Mail delivery was halted. Professional baseball and basketball games were canceled. Los Angeles Unified School District officials decided to close every school and child-care center. At Cal State and USC, where a bunch of college kids were getting ready to finish their year, all the exams were canceled, and the college actually hired a bunch of runners to go classroom to classroom to tell everybody to get out and get home while they still could. Big companies in downtown Los Angeles had to let thousands of employees leave work early so they could get home before it got dark. Those who went to work huddled around radios, took calls from worried relatives and friends, and watched from their high-rise offices as smoke rose over the entire city. All the big theater shows and cultural events were canceled.

One South Los Angeles woman told county officials that her husband's kidney dialysis machine wouldn't work with the power outages. The utility company had told her it was too dangerous to send out a repairman. Paramedics finally arrived to provide a portable dialysis unit, only to have it run out of fuel.

Our society was broken. The world around me looked like a natural disaster. Except we had done this to ourselves, made our world just fall apart.

And I couldn't help but feel the burden for what was happening and it was devastating to me.

MILITARY MIGHT—OR MIGHT NOT

The government couldn't begin to handle the mob violence. And I believe that the police, although ordered to pull back, couldn't have handled it, even if they had been allowed to try. There's no way around the fact that for a whole day, the authorities just let L.A. burn. Recently it felt like they did the same thing in New Orleans, just let the poor bastards get sick, drown, or starve.

Local police departments were swamped with calls, but they couldn't respond if they were in areas that were too dangerous. When the National Guard finally arrived from upstate at the command of Governor Wilson, the troops sat for the whole day in their barracks. They didn't get the proper orders, or the right person didn't tell them where to go, they said. And they didn't have enough bullets. I don't know how many bullets they thought they needed, but I guess their regular supply wasn't enough. I believe that showed us how frightened everybody was. As the troops waited to deploy, they spent time in last-minute training exercises and briefings on crowd control.

We heard there were about a hundred or so soldiers in camouflage up at the armory near Brookhurst Road and Valencia Drive in Fullerton. They were cleaning automatic rifles, sheathing bayonets, checking gas masks, face shields, helmets. Behind the armory, the soldiers practiced crowd-control techniques, using three-foot-long wooden clubs attached to leather straps. They'd stand shoulder-to-shoulder, holding the clubs with both hands in front of their chests. It was a little late for practice. But they must have been scared too, I guess. We all were. At some staging points in the county, one of the guards admitted that they were all ill prepared and said that street duty for riots worried them more than being called up for the Gulf War.

Finally, nearly a day after the whole thing started, some of those Guard units finally deployed. As the day wore on, and the looting and violence got worse and worse, we all started asking questions. Why had nobody come to help? Why didn't the troops make it to the streets sooner? I really think that frustration was part of what kept the riots going so long—the feeling that nobody cared anyway. It just made people more angry.

Meanwhile, everybody I knew was getting out their guns and locking their doors, even covering their cars with tarps or blankets to keep the ash off, and to be a little less tempting to somebody angry with a brick in their hand. If they didn't have guns, they went to buy them at local gun shops and pawn shops. They probably all got turned away unarmed, because State law said you couldn't buy a gun in just one day. Besides that, the city put out an emergency order saying nobody could buy ammo or used handguns. L.A. officials said they were trying to keep people from accidentally shooting each other or police during the rioting. But there were plenty of gun stores that ignored the new rule, as well as lots of stores in other nearby cities. They sold out fast. People bought whatever ammunition was available—even if they didn't have a gun. They were hoping that they could use it to barter for guns from neighbors and friends.

Desperation drove these people to want guns. And for most of them, it wasn't to go rob and steal. If the police weren't going to protect their families and children, everybody would have to protect themselves. This was one of the saddest things about violence, that it turned everybody away from his fellow man. Made us all feel alone. And the more afraid we felt, the more we wanted to lash out at anybody who wasn't just like us.

I felt very sorry for all those business owners. They were just innocent people working hard to make money and take care of themselves and their families. They definitely got the worst of it. If you owned a store in Los Angeles, you were certainly going to be nervous. A bunch of the liquor store and grocery store owners all got together in Koreatown, along with some owners of restaurants and dry cleaners, and they mobilized their own army. You could see them on television in open shoot-outs with looters. There, on television, right in front of me, I saw a liquor store I used to go to burning to the ground. I saw a couple of fast-food restaurants and grocery stores I used to drive by all the time, and they were just crushed, like a wrecking ball had been dropped on them. The entire structure had been torn down.

I sat in front of the television and put my head in my hands. All my memories returned of me riding my bike when I was a kid, and running through back alleys and jumping fences, memories of swimming and fishing, and just being a kid in L.A. And I kept thinking, what if there is nothing left for my kids? I thought about how the violence was just spreading, like the seasonal wildfires. Interstate 280 had to be closed, and California 1, and the whole San Francisco–Oakland Bay Bridge. It was like California was breaking off from the USA and sinking.

I'd never really given much thought to being a kid born in Sacramento, California, and living in Los Angeles. But watching it all get crushed, it made me feel for the first time like this was my city, like it was a part of me. And because of that, I needed to do something to save it.

ON THE THIRD DAY

When I got a call from my lawyer, Steven Lerman, I immediately knew what he wanted, and I knew how I'd respond. He and Tom Owens, the investigator, asked me to come forward and say something to calm things down. When I told Momma what he was asking for, she tried to make me promise to lay low.

She became very frightened for me and said, "Don't do nothing. Nothing!" She begged me. "You had your time in the spotlight, and it done you no good. Now just promise me you'll say nothing. Promise me!"

Momma said that no matter what I said, I was going to piss off a bunch of people, and that it would do no good to me, no way. I had to admit, she made a lot of sense.

I understood she was trying to protect me and all, but by the third day, the riots had just gotten so out of hand that I knew I would never be able to live with myself if I didn't do something. They were saying that over fifty people had been killed, and over two thousand injured. I felt like I could barely breathe, the whole thing was weighing so heavily on me. So I did my own little gut check and told myself I could do this. In fact a part of me had been preparing for this, even though I truly dreaded it. I called Steve back and asked him where we should meet.

Steve and Tom looked extremely serious when I showed up. The press was already there, and they just swarmed me. The thing was, when I joined up with Steve, he had a whole long, four-page prepared statement for me to read.

I took one look at those four pages and said fuck that. They were insisting I read what they wrote, but I was going to speak my own words. Without consciously realizing it, I had been working on what I would say about the riots probably since the first brick was thrown. I knew this was true because when I got up there to speak, it felt like I had already run certain words over and over in my head.

God knows I wanted to help, I really did. My mind never had the proper schooling to do what I was about to do, but that was okay because these words were coming from my heart. I had a real powerful desire to say something that might stick, might make an impression and do some good.

But when I got up there, and the TV lights went on, and the recorders started whirring and cameras snapping, a lot of what I was about to say flew out of my head. I was not the ideal guy for this, but thankfully enough words stayed with me, and every word I spoke was as true as I could make it and came right out of a deep place in my heart and soul. There was nothing but the best intentions behind everything I said. For the first time in my life, I realized ain't none of us going to make it in this world unless we figure out a way to do it together.

So I began, "People, I just want to say, can we all get along? Can we get along? . . . We've just got to, just got to. We're all stuck here for a while. . . . Let's try to work it out. Let's try to work it out."

AFTERMATH

I wish I could say that I was so good at speaking that everybody listened and everything got peaceful and quiet. But reality is a bitch and it took a while. A couple more days were pretty rough and then everything finally calmed down. By then, thousands of the men and women who were in the mobs and riots were now in courthouses. They got charged with looting, arson, assault—all sorts of stuff. From Wednesday to the next Friday, police said they arrested close to eighteen thousand people.

One month later, justice became a crapshoot for most of those eighteen thousand. The court system proved to be what it was, a kind of joke. That didn't surprise me a bit. Some people who stole got one-year jail terms in one set of courts, but at another they got off with community service. They all flooded the court system and overran jail space. So judges started making deals. In return for guilty pleas, accused folks could pick from a menu of three sentences: thirty days in jail, three hundred hours of community service, or thirty days of work on a Caltrans cleanup crew. You gotta do what you gotta do, but the whole thing just made it more clear to everybody that justice was always a bit of a crapshoot, and you never knew how the dice would land.

President Bush came to L.A. with a tough message: "Lawlessness . . . must be punished." His visits to a disaster assistance center and speeches to business and political leaders seemed kind of slick and rehearsed, but at least he was there to urge all of us to soldier on. Nothing could change the facts, though. We had seen the anger and rage at the heart of our city. It all came pouring out of everybody, and just because the fires were out didn't mean the hatred and resentment had ended.

A couple months later, I woke up one morning feeling like the whole thing had been a bad dream. It felt like it never happened. But then you'd drive by a charred, empty lot where a store once stood and all the sickening images would come flooding back. You'd get to the 7-Eleven and see the Reginald Denny trial on the front page of the paper, then run into somebody who was just getting out of jail for assault, or see someone who had a cousin who was caught in crossfire on the second day. And just like that it was right back in my face.

Chapter 4

A SECOND CHANCE AT JUSTICE

THE FEDERAL TRIAL

The riots changed everything. Even now, ask anybody and they'll remember where they were when they heard about the acquittal of the four police officers and how the city erupted. Everybody kind of raised their eyebrows in surprise and then shook their heads in disbelief. For some, that was about the extent of their reaction, but for many others, it triggered a long simmering resentment that led to an outpouring of rage.

It was not just people in L.A. who were dealing with the crazy verdict and the even crazier riots, but people everywhere, all the way up to President George H. W. Bush. I admit I hadn't been much of a supporter of his, though I felt patriotic as hell during the Gulf War. But after the verdict had come down and the riots exploded across the city, I was happy to hear that he had the courage to speak up.

"I will do my level best to heal the wounds and bring people together in the aftermath of the ugliness we witnessed last night," he said. "A president should do no less."

After the sheer disbelief and overwhelming sadness I felt after the verdict, I knew if I was going to have a chance to see that justice was done, someone high up in the system would have to be outraged enough to take on my cause. Many people don't understand how those policemen ended up back in a courtroom again after that "not guilty" verdict came down. The fact is that a lot, or maybe all, of the civil trial had to do with President Bush and his insistence that justice be done. I still think about him and how his direct involvement helped all of us in this country feel like we could maybe trust the judicial system, that it actually worked.

President Bush was so concerned that he called Mayor Tom Bradley and Governor Pete Wilson and offered them federal assistance. And even though Bradley and Wilson were knee-deep in the riots at the time, they claimed they didn't know the full extent of the toll, so they didn't know exactly what kind of help to ask for. At least that's what I was told.

The violence triggered by the verdict took the president completely by surprise. He didn't seem to have his finger on the pulse of the racial tension in L.A. Looking back, historians have noted that lack of awareness was probably due to cutbacks during the previous administration under President Reagan. Arthur Fletcher, who was chairman of the U.S. Commission on Civil Rights under Bush, pointed out that when Reagan was president, the commission was "decimated." To make matters worse, the Reagan Administration had also downsized the Community Relations Service over at the justice department, which was supposed to keep an eye on race relations throughout the country. As a result, there wasn't much information on the racial tensions that led to the L.A. riots. So when Fletcher met with Bradley after I was beaten by the cops to discuss the racial issues of the city, I believe he wasn't properly prepared.

By that point, the federal government was desperate to be thoroughly and accurately briefed on the situation. Fletcher wasn't just worried about L.A. He said the Civil Rights Commission had plenty of reports citing other cities as "tinderboxes" of racial tension. The federal government was afraid that L.A. was just the beginning, and it was taking this threat seriously. Bush met with black leaders to talk about the situation. Coretta Scott King, Martin's widow, and the heads of the NAACP and the National Urban League were among those in the room with Bush. In my opinion, the black leaders should have held their own meeting and invited Bush.

The president was not happy with the acquittal of the four officers, and he certainly wasn't pleased with the riots either. He called the violence in L.A. "purely criminal," "mob brutality," and "wanton destruction." He said, "We simply cannot condone violence as a way of changing the system." He insisted that "we must stand up against lawlessness and crime, wherever it takes place." Man, I couldn't have agreed more with the president's stand against violence. I said so then, and I've been saying so ever since.

CIVIL RIGHTS

While he was denouncing what was happening in the streets, President Bush went beyond lip service. He ordered the justice department to look into the possibility of federal prosecution of the acquitted cops on the charge of violating my civil rights. Civil rights leaders and members of Congress had made it clear that they were angry about the acquittals—and they wanted the justice department to do something. Jesse Jackson and Representative Maxine Waters were among those applying political pressure. Jackson and Waters met with the attorney general at the time, William P. Barr, and urged him not to waste time when it came to slapping federal charges on the four cops.

"We let them [A. G. Barr and the Department of Justice] know that we think the situation not only in Los Angeles but across the nation is extremely volatile," Waters said. "And we want them to make the decision with all due haste."

Jackson didn't hold back. He took the occasion to really tear into Bush. He severely criticized the president's leadership of the country and said that Bush was siding with L.A. Police Chief Darryl F. Gates. Jackson thought Bush and Gates were acting like buddies, which made the president seem to Jackson like he had a "disregard for justice and fairness." Maybe it was just sour grapes because Jackson had wanted to meet with Bush the night after the riots erupted, but Bush had declined. He had to go to a state dinner, so he didn't have time for a face-to-face with Jackson then. But other civil rights leaders throughout the nation also pointed a finger at Bush for not

Asking for peace during a press conference in Los Angeles, May 1, 1992.

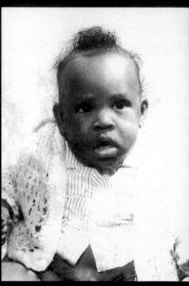

Top left: My brother Gailen with his son.
Top right: Eight months old, 1965.
Above: The King boys.

Top: Pumping iron at Fire Camp, Pasadena, 1990.
Above: My brother Paul, 17, with the catch of the day.

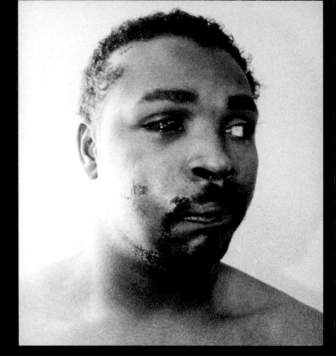

LOVE YOUR NE
- J
WE CAN GET
- RODNE

Top: Still mending after the beating.
Above: Asian American demonstrators march through the
streets of Los Angeles, May 1992.

Top: Leaving the courthouse after attending a preliminary hearing.

A hug with Rosa Parks, 1992.

Top: My grandmother, Elizabeth. She was always the life of the party!! I loved her so much.
Above: A visit from my mom and two of my uncles, Stanley and Wesley. I'm holding my daughter Tristan here.

Ready to rap!

RODNEY G. KING

CEO

Top: Here I am with my nieces Britney and Tasha, my daughter Tristan, and my mom, Odessa.

Above: Big smiles from my brother, Juan and Mom.

Top: Fishing at Puddenstone Lake, 2011.
Above: Holiday with my family, Thanksgiving, 2010.

Top: With my girls—daughters Deana, Tristan, and Candance.
Above: My favorite place to be—outdoors.

Top: Celebrity Boxing event at the Avalon, with Cynthia and Nadya Sulman (Octomom). *Above:* Cynthia and me on our way to a BET event for 50 Greatest African Americans, 2011.

Top: Kim Fields, me, Queen Latifah, and my brother, Paul. Queen Latifah invited us to drop by when she was working on *Living Single.* She inspired me to kickstart my label.
Above: Signing autographs at Franklin Elementary, Altadena

A new man.

moving quickly enough when it came to dealing with the mess in Los Angeles.

But the Department of Justice didn't just pound the podium. It tried to assure the public that it was actually doing its part to handle the volatile situation following the verdict as quickly as possible. It opened a civil rights investigation and held a news conference, during which one of the spokesmen said, "It's important for people to understand that the verdicts yesterday on state charges are not the end of the process." The spokesman said the DOJ would "vigorously" enforce the nation's civil rights laws. They tried to show they meant business by having then FBI Director William S. Sessions and then Assistant Attorney General for Civil Rights John R. Dunne show up at the news conference. This gave my family hope that there might still be justice for what those officers did to me.

The DOJ hadn't been completely absent in the picture before the riots. It had an ear to the ground in L.A. during the state trial against the four cops. It had several conciliation specialists, as the DOJ called them, in town while the trial was going on. These representatives were in touch with local officials and leaders of community and civic groups to assess and try to handle the racial situation.

It became clear to most of us pretty quickly that the DOJ's role wouldn't be limited to trying to smooth things over among the various racial communities in the city. That's what you do when it's just an average day. This was not an average day. What the federal government had in its hands was a potential national crisis. And most Americans were scratching their heads about the question of justice. On top of that, there were people out looting and rioting and setting fires in public, spreading from neighborhood to neighborhood. There was a real and rational fear that this violence could spread, potentially from city to city, then state to state. The federal government decided it couldn't just stand by any longer.

THE DECISION

It took a while for the DOJ to decide what they were going to do. A whole summer, actually. All those weeks after the riots, while the days grew longer and kids got out of school, I remember waking up every day wondering where the story might spread to next.

I was still meeting with my attorneys all the time, but I couldn't get any real answers about what action the DOJ would probably take. It wasn't the lawyers' fault—I don't think anybody knew what the DOJ would do, or if these officers would actually ever see another day in court. There was still so much anger in the city, still so many people pissed off about what they'd seen happen, it really felt like the whole thing could explode again. All it would take was one nervous cop and one imposing lawbreaker running into each other and the whole city might just go up in flames again. Those weeks passed slowly, that's for sure. It seemed like the longest summer of my life.

The DOJ finally decided to prosecute Koon, Powell, Briseno, and Wind on federal civil rights charges. On August 4, 1992, a federal grand jury indictment came down on them. And all of a sudden, I found myself spending my days in the courtroom again. As glad as I was that we had the chance to revisit the actions of the police involved, I was nervous, too. It might have seemed like an open-and-shut case to everybody on the streets. It sure seemed simple to me: what they'd done to me was wrong, and they deserved to be punished for it. But in that courtroom, everything became more complicated.

FEDERAL TRUMPS STATE

In the state trial, the prosecution had to prove that the cops acted with criminal intent. But this time, the federal government had to prove that the cops had violated my civil rights by intentionally using excessive force. Koon's charge was a bit different from that of the other three cops in the federal trial. Because of his senior authority over the other officers at the incident, he was indicted for violating my civil rights by not stopping the beating once it had started.

The media game started right away. Harland Braun, Briseno's lawyer, said federal prosecution was a blatant political decision. "This is a political case, not a legal case," he said. Briseno couldn't believe he was back on trial. "I'm upset. I'm angry. I'm hurt," he said. "I don't understand why. Everybody viewed the video. There's no question what role I played in it." He insisted, "I tried to stop it. I don't know why they're putting me through this again." Braun speculated that Briseno was indicted because the government wanted testimony from him against the other cops but didn't want to give him immunity. Like Briseno, Powell also couldn't believe he had to face court again. He repeated what he'd always been saying about the beating: "I did what I was supposed to do." All four officers faced up to ten years behind bars and $250,000 in fines if they were convicted this time.

Despite all the protests from the officers involved and their lawyers, the federal prosecutors were confident about their chances of getting convictions. In general, federal prosecutors have an easier time getting convictions in police brutality cases because of a civil rights law that dates from right after the Civil War, a law that had actually been passed to hold accountable members of the Ku Klux Klan and the police for mistreating blacks. Plus, unlike state governments, the federal government had a dedicated civil rights legal team. The federal prosecutors had a powerful law behind them, and a lot of resources.

In all, the federal government had fifteen or so lawyers and a team of FBI agents on the case. The public faces of the prosecution were two DOJ lawyers, Barry Kowalski and Steven Clymer. Kowalski had a reputation for being a heavy hitter when it came to civil rights. He had a long list of racists that he had previously prosecuted, including neo-Nazis, Klansmen, and skinheads. Clymer was known as a star in the L.A. U.S. attorney's office. He used to lead the U.S. Attorney's Office Major Crimes Division, and he was a pro at handling high-profile cases. Both Barry Kowalski and Steve Clymer were handpicked to be the federal prosecutors in this case. I liked the feds immediately. They had a swagger and confidence to them that was really reassuring. Kowalski and Clymer said they were not sure how many they were going to get, but they were going to make sure someone was held responsible. I liked the fact that they told me they didn't come down to L.A. to be my friend but to make sure that justice was served.

The two lawyers felt good about the possibility of winning, but they weren't arrogant about it. I know I sure felt like nothing was a sure thing. In the state trial, they had shown the videotape of my beating over and over again. I honestly don't know how many times that gruesome scene was replayed. But evidently it wasn't enough to convict the four officers! If that hard evidence failed to put these guys in jail, then what would? I kept hearing it was going to be a case we could win, but I admit I wasn't really that confident at all. Kowalski and Clymer knew they had a hard road ahead of them. The federal case was more complicated than the state case because the feds had to show two things: that the cops had used excessive force against me and that they did so with the intention of violating my civil rights.

On the defense side, the officers were represented by Ira Salzman for Koon, Michael P. Stone for Powell, Paul DePasquale for Wind, and Harland W. Braun for Briseno. They had so many lawyers, consultants, and experts on this or that around them, I couldn't hardly tell who was who. But it was obvious that Stone and Braun were the big shots of the defense. Stone used to be a cop, and he was the most outspoken defense lawyer during the state trial. Braun also liked to stand out. He was famous for being a criminal defense lawyer in L.A., and he liked to get loud in court. It was part of his act, I suppose. He even got a bit out of hand, and U.S. District Judge John G. Davies, who was presiding over the federal case, tried to restrain him with a partial gag order, which was later overturned.

Just like in the state trial, the defendants were left to fight each other. Briseno wanted Stone removed from the trial, and he filed a motion saying that Stone had a conflict of interest. Stone was a lawyer for the Los Angeles Police Protective League, and Briseno was part of the league, which meant that Stone was technically his lawyer. But Briseno accused Stone of attacking his defense at the state trial, when Briseno separated himself from the other cops by saying he tried to stop the beating. Stone had cops come into the courtroom to testify *against* Briseno! It was crazy. I couldn't believe it. It was almost like Stone was trying to enforce the code of silence among police officers. Braun, Briseno's lawyer, said removing Stone from the federal case would allow Briseno to have a chance at a fair trial.

It was very clear that Briseno was trying to separate himself from the other three cops. It appeared that he didn't want to be associated with them at all. Koon shot back at him by filing a motion to remove Briseno from the trial because of "antagonistic defenses." Briseno asked for the case against him to be dismissed altogether. He said he shouldn't be on trial because he didn't use excessive force on me.

FEAR FACTOR

But, in fairness, the officer did add, "I wish to emphasize to the court that I do not believe that any of my co-defendants are guilty," he said. "I do not believe they acted with a criminal intent in applying force to Mr. King." Briseno believed the cops didn't mean to beat me that night. They only did it because they were afraid of me. Braun interpreted for Briseno, saying he "has always felt it was excessive force, but not with intent, just fear."

I always believed this fear factor defense could not possibly justify their actions for the entire duration of the arrest. How many bones did they have to break, how many quarts of blood did I have to lose before their fear died down? After forty plus baton blows, after a dozen kicks to the head, neck, and testicles, after not one but two Taser electrocutions, how could they possibly justify continuing to mutilate me because they were still afraid of me?

This tactic of claiming fear was becoming old news to me. It was my understanding that by insisting they were in fear of their lives, the officers could sidestep the whole race issue. It's just like the tried-and-true PCP tactic. It's common knowledge that whenever the cops used the choke hold to subdue a suspect who was resisting arrest and that person was left in critical condition, a coma, or died on them, the officer would claim that the suspect behaved extremely violently and was capable of inflicting mortal wounds because he was high on

PCP. No jury would contest that, and it became a guaranteed ticket to freedom for the law enforcement officer accused.

Despite what I wanted, and what I thought was fair, I would have been an idiot to not see what Briseno was thinking. I'll tell you what he was thinking: he was worried about the riots. He didn't believe that he'd get a fair trial because the jury would be afraid of potentially fueling more riots with another "not guilty" verdict. Briseno said that jurors would be crazy not to declare the officers guilty because the jurors would naturally fear for their lives and the lives of other citizens. I'd been thinking the exact same thing. In fact, that's most likely what we were all worried about.

It took another six months to get to trial, and by the time it began, it had been nearly a year since the state trial began. Things move awfully slow in the legal system. I was involved as much as I could be, but even I went weeks without knowing what was going on, or what could possibly be holding things up.

While the lawyers got all their papers organized and started up the big machine that was the federal courts, I spent my days working out. I loved going bike riding and jogging to stay in shape, and even went skiing with my attorney Grimes up at Mammoth Mountain and Lake Tahoe. All of this activity, however, was very limited because I was still on the mend and at any time, a severe headache could come along and leave me completely sidelined for the morning or afternoon.

The trial opened on February 25, 1993. Stone remained Powell's lawyer, and Briseno remained a defendant. The presiding judge was Davies, a 1986 Reagan appointee who also

presided in my later civil lawsuit against L.A. and the officers.
I believe Judge Davies tried to be fair and balanced. He had a
reputation for being moderate and conservative, but also independent and open-minded. He wanted to make sure the jurors
had complete anonymity, so he sequestered them and ordered
artists in the courtroom not to sketch their faces. The jury in
this trial had nine whites, two blacks, and one Hispanic. That
was better than the one-sided composition of the first jury, but
still seemed unbalanced.

Clymer made waves by sharing the story of how the cops
had blatantly showed me off around the precinct police station
in my beat-up state. I had been suffering from multiple fractures to my skull and legs, and instead of rushing me between
hospitals, they were gloating, letting their fellow cops see their
handiwork. The cops had first taken me to Pacifica Hospital,
and I was supposed to then go to Los Angeles County–USC
Medical Center's jail ward. But the cops took about a two-hour
pit stop. Clymer said Powell drove to his Foothill Division
station and called officers to come out and see me. I was in
the backseat of a cop car with Wind. Clymer said that Powell
"sent police officers out to look at Rodney King while Rodney
King was in the back seat, waiting for medical attention." Not
only did they delay getting me the medical attention I needed,
they also lied on their police report. Clymer pointed out that
the report wrongly stated they left Pacifica Hospital at four
forty-five in the morning. The correct time was three thirty
A.M. "They omit completely on that log that they ever went to
Foothill station."

The Foothill stop in between hospitals was new information. It hadn't been brought up in the state case at all. An L.A. county official said the prosecution in the state case had never known about it. If prosecutors had evidence of it back then, "We would have presented it," said the official.

Stone dealt with Clymer's attack by saying the trip to the Foothill station was made so the cops could pave the way for booking me into the L.A. USC Med Center's jail ward. He also said the cops weren't aware that I had been badly injured. That was ridiculous because I remember almost passing out in the back seat of the black-and-white, and they knew that if I lay down, my throat could fill with blood and I would have suffocated. So they put an officer in the back seat with me who kept propping my head up so I wouldn't die. Stone downplayed my injuries by saying that the report from the doctor who treated me at Pacifica didn't say anything about serious injuries. The report just said the doctor treated me for "superficial lacerations," which basically meant the visible cuts on the skin, and that I was given something for "PCP overdose." Stone also suggested that if I were that seriously injured, I would've left Pacifica in an ambulance. But I didn't. I left in a police car. Really? But that was their decision, not mine or a doctor's.

It didn't take long before the videotape of the beating was brought out again. Man, I was so sick of watching it. Over and over and over. Like it was the only moment of my life. Clymer showed it at regular speed and then again and again in slow motion. He'd take it section by section, so he could detail the blows. He wanted to show that "this case involves police brutality." Clymer said, "The Los Angeles Police Department trains its officers that unless their lives are threatened, they cannot use a baton to strike a suspect in the face or head." Medical experts testified about the repeated blows the cops struck on my head and face. One of the experts was Harry L. Smith, who specialized in biomechanics. He brought in all kinds of stuff to explain to the jury what he wanted them to believe. He had X-rays, a head mockup, photos, a plastic skull, and other props to make his case. The prosecution also had an LAPD use-of-force expert, Sergeant Mark Conta. He testified that the four cops had violated LAPD policy when they hit me. The prosecution tried to show that Powell hit me in the head two to four times. If the hits were intentional, then they would have been against LAPD policy.

It might sound crazy, but the longer I was in the courtroom during all these trials, and the more witnesses I heard and the more I saw that tape, the more unreal it all seemed to be. I had moments when I couldn't believe it had all actually happened to me. After a while, it was like they were talking about somebody else. Like when you say a word over and over again and it somehow starts to sound weird and loses its meaning. It was like that. There were some moments when I didn't feel like the Rodney King they were talking about was me at all. I remember the pain of all those blows. And in my head I can still hear the shouts of the police officers. But so much of it seems like a bad dream, like it had to have happened to somebody else. Maybe this was part of a defense mechanism for my healing, I just don't know.

The defense also used the videotape of the beating, but Stone argued that my injuries didn't come from getting hit by batons. He said my head injuries were the result of me falling down face-first on the pavement several times. Then he brought in doctors to testify to this version of events. "This incident, far from being an out-of-control beating of a motorist, was a controlled use of force," said Stone. "In a sense, it is the suspect who is in control."

What? That comment seemed to cross the line into the twilight zone. Why didn't he just say that I was into self-mutilation because I thought it would get the cops in more trouble? In a sense, this notion was just insane, and I just started crying when I heard that. I'm a fighter. And there's not one time you will see me willingly slam my head into the pavement. I had to be pushed, beaten, or Tasered into it.

Both Stone and Salzman denied that Powell and Koon had filed false police reports. Stone thought he had an ace in the hole. He had Timothy and Melanie Singer, two of the California Highway Patrol officers who chased me the night of the beating, and Bryant Allen, one of the guys in my car that night, as witnesses. This was a surprise, because these three people had been witnesses for the prosecution in the state case. The accounts they gave in the state trial didn't match up with each other. "They did so well for us last time, I figured we should call them," Stone said about having the three on the defense side this time around. Salzman had his own trick up his sleeve: one of his witnesses was Sergeant Conta's teacher.

A key witness for the prosecution that the state didn't have was me. It was pure torture having to stay at home and not be permitted, by my lawyers, to enter the courtroom for the entire duration of the first trial. They may as well have kept me cuffed in the backseat of that black and white. But that wouldn't be a problem this time. I was put on the stand. They were going to talk to me and I was going to be able to look the lawyer and the jury right in the face and give my answers. Thank god the feds weren't afraid to use me. I was ready and relieved, because my experience was that the lawyers want all the attention; they want everyone to focus during a trial on themselves. I was honestly glad that they called me up there.

Every day when the feds picked me up, they had an officer beside me who was wearing a bulletproof vest. They'd walk me through the parking garage into the courthouse, where I sat silently, watching a lot of other people talk about me and what happened to me. Over and over again, they mentioned my name—"Mr. King"—and over and over again, they explained where I was, who had hit me, and what happened.

By March 1993, I finally got to speak for myself. It felt good to be on that stand, answering questions about that night. Telling my own story. I only got to tell it to a hundred people or so, but it still felt great. The court had banned all cameras, and even all recording devices. So it was just me and that courtroom and whoever had gotten a seat to the show. But even with just that small crowd, it felt good to finally represent myself and use my voice.

The room was so quiet. There was always some rustling when other people were on the stand. Lawyers talking. Consultants coming and going; people generally moving and shifting. But when I was up there, it was quiet as a church. You could hear a pin drop when I took the stand. At least that's how I remember it. I had been waiting for this moment for a long time, because I felt like I was finally able to tell my story. This, I realized, was the reason I had ordered myself to stay alive that night, so that one day, I would be heard.

Clymer was brilliant because he didn't try to hide my wrongdoing the night of the beating. He was honest with the jury about my being drunk, being on parole, and speeding as I was trying to get away from the police. But he said, "Rodney King is not on trial." Powell, Koon, Wind, and Briseno were.

Putting me on the stand definitely helped the prosecution. Salzman said I came off as "a regular guy." I told the court I felt abused on the night of the beating. "I felt like my blood was boiling inside of me," I said. "I felt horrible. I felt in lots of pain and I was wondering what did I do to deserve that type of pain." Clymer asked me about what I remembered, and I told him as honestly as I could about that night. Each baton hit and boot kick, each word I remembered the officers screaming at me, "You better run. We're going to kill you. We're going to kill you, nigger, run!" It was tough to describe it all, but I did my best. The *New York Times* said: "Far from the image of a 'drug-crazed giant' evoked by lawyers defending four police officers accused of violating his civil rights, Mr. King's demeanor was meek and earnest." I didn't try to be anything up there but myself.

The way everybody acted when I took the stand was the way I acted when Dorothy Gibson took the stand. I was silent and listened hard to her. She was just a bystander who witnessed the beating, but after hearing so many doctors and lawyers talk about that night, it was emotional for me to hear it from someone who was there, and who had no particular agenda or expertise. Gibson had seen the beating from across the street, and she was clearly still disturbed by it when she was on the stand. She almost cried. She said my "hands were stretched out like a cross shape" while the cops were hitting me.

VERDICT AND VINDICATION

I had my twenty-eighth birthday as the case was wrapping up, but we decided to hold off with any celebration. In the end, the prosecution made a very compelling case. In my opinion, they were intelligent, determined attorneys. The jury spent about a week deliberating, and on April 17, 1993, they found Koon and Powell guilty of violating my civil rights. Wind and Briseno were found not guilty.

That day, I felt that justice was half served. And I know that change, particularly change for good, is always slow. But I was at peace after the verdict, and it was the nicest birthday gift I'd gotten in a long time.

Everybody said that Los Angeles breathed a sigh of relief when the verdict was handed down. I know that's definitely true. During that whole week, it was like we were all holding our breath. What if they were acquitted again? Would the city burst open? Even New York City started airing a bunch of television and radio commercials encouraging racial tolerance and goodwill in the days leading up to the jury's decision. I was nervous too. For my city, yes. But also for me. I didn't know what I'd do if another court said the cops were innocent. I honestly felt I might lose my mind if I heard that. It would be like the world telling me I made the whole thing up. Like the video didn't matter or even exist. Like I didn't matter or exist, either.

THE SENTENCE

It was up to Judge Davies to determine Koon's and Powell's sentences. "The task is not an easy one," he said. "I have tried to treat all of the participants, not as symbols, but as individuals." At the sentence hearing, Davies emphasized the humanity of Koon and Powell. He said Koon is a dad, an Air Force vet, and a "successful police officer with an extraordinary record." As for Powell, Davies said he has "a family where he has enjoyed the strong support of his parents and four brothers and sisters." Judge Davies didn't have such great things to say about me. He said I had provoked the beating. I had no choice but to sit there and take it, a situation that I was becoming painfully used to by then.

The judge decided that most of the baton blows were legal because I was resisting arrest and the police were trying to subdue me. Davies said only about six hits by Powell were considered excessive use of force, because those hits were done when I was already supposedly subdued. Davies also took into account the personal suffering of the officers, that their careers and their lives were basically a wreck.

The prosecution wanted Powell to get seven to nine years and Koon to get nine to ten years behind bars. Prosecutors also wanted them to pay fines and to pay me restitution. Davies didn't agree. The judge sentenced Powell and Koon to thirty months each in prison and didn't order them to pay anything except $50 each for a special court assessment.

Some of the blacks in L.A. complained that Powell and Koon got off easy with a sentence of only two and a half years. The president of the NAACP's L.A. chapter, Joseph Duff, said, "This is a travesty of justice as opposed to a measure of justice." One of the jurors, Erik Rasmussen, also thought Powell and Koon should've gotten more prison time. He said, "I didn't think the punishment fit the crime." He thought the two should've been sentenced to five to seven years in prison.

Koon's and Powell's lawyers had wanted the officers to get less than a year behind bars or get probation, but they didn't argue with the judge's call. "It is harsh," Stone said of the two-and-a-half-year sentences. "But it is harsh because the law requires it."

There were some serious fears of another riot being sparked by the outcome of this trial, and the LAPD was put on high alert. But the city stayed quiet. Mayor Richard Riordan gave a speech live on TV right after Judge Davies handed down his sentences. He asked the city to move on. "The judicial system worked," he said, "maybe not the way that many of us would like it to have worked, but it did work."

The prosecution didn't think the thirty-month sentences were sufficient punishment. U.S. Attorney Terree A. Bowers said in a statement that: "The government, in its sentencing memorandum, argued that the sentencing guidelines mandated substantially higher prison terms for both defendants," and "We are disappointed by the downward departures imposed today."

On August 27, 1993, the Department of Justice publicly stated that it would appeal Koon's and Powell's sentences. The DOJ wanted the two officers to serve more than thirty months in prison. In October 1993, the two began serving their sentences. The Ninth Circuit Court of Appeals sided with the DOJ in January 1995, and ruled that the sentences were not long enough. Koon and Powell appealed the Ninth Circuit's ruling, and the Supreme Court decided in September 1995 to hear their appeal. Judge Davies was put back on the case, and he was supposed to give them a tougher sentence. Powell and Koon got out of prison in December 1995. In June 1996, the Supreme Court reversed the Ninth Circuit's ruling but also ordered Davies to resentence Powell and Koon. Davies put an end to the whole thing in September 1996 by sticking to his original sentence and refusing to order more prison time be served by the two officers.

RACIALLY MOTIVATED

Some said it was finally over. But the honest truth is that it's never over. Because until we do away with the prejudice and racism that fueled that horrific night, hate-motivated arrests will continue, as we have witnessed during the last twenty years, to cloud law enforcement.

Can anyone in law enforcement be a racist and still do their job? Can anyone in the judicial system be prejudiced and still uphold the law fairly? Maybe we just have to keep doing what Warren Beatty's character proclaimed in his film *Bulworth*. He encouraged interracial marriages so that one blessed day, one perfect day, we will all look the same. Then there will be no racism, because there will only be one race.

As for our justice system, I received a crash course in legal representation rivaled by no one. My on-the-job experience and training, however, came at a steep price. I had to bob, weave, duck, and dive through a platoon of lawyers, each with their own outsized ego and personal agenda. It proved to be as challenging as the trials themselves, and some more hard lessons were in store for me. I am sometimes embarrassed by how clueless I was when dealing with attorneys and our justice system. But my main flaw was that I was trusting, and believed that because I was asking them to represent me and paying them to go to bat for me, I could think of them as brothers-in-arms and, in some cases, as brothers. I was in for one rude, painful, and disappointing awakening.

Along with these difficult lessons, I began to realize that complaining about being deceived and mislead was just an excuse for not taking full responsibility for what was happening in my own life. I had to start being more accountable, but I was nowhere near that realization yet.

Chapter 5

HATE AND CONFUSION

POLITICS AND THE CIVIL TRIAL

The beating caused the city to take a hard look at its police department, and there was no way the LAPD was getting off easy this time. Police Chief Darryl Gates, a white Republican who was responsible for the officers' conduct on the field, was the obvious target. When the beating became public, Mayor Tom Bradley, a black Democrat, kept quiet at first about what to do with Chief Gates, who was known for his tough stance on law enforcement and aggressive enforcement policies. Gates started on the police force in 1949, and during his time as police chief, L.A.'s population had grown to twice the size it was since he was a rookie cop. L.A. also had a serious spike in crime over those years. Drugs and gang violence became a big problem, and Gates dealt with it by shaking things up in the police force. He put more cops out on the streets and increased surveillance in the city. No one could say he wasn't tough on crime.

Bradley didn't know what to do with Gates yet, so any disciplinary steps just sat festering. The mayor only stated that

Gates "has to answer to his public." Then Bradley changed his mind. By April 1991, Bradley called on attorney Warren Christopher to shine a light on the LAPD and launch a formal investigation. They called it the Christopher Commission, which wasted no time in coming out with a report in July of 1991 that said it would be best for Gates to step down. The report had identified a "significant number" of cops who had a habit of using excessive force, and these cops often targeted minorities. But I think the cops got away with it most of the time because they wrote up their police reports to make sure they could not be accused of a racially motivated arrest. But there were cops who sent private messages with racist remarks to other cops. The report also found that the LAPD was lagging behind the PD's in other large cities at hiring minorities and promoting them.

Gates called my beating from the cops an "aberration." And obviously a lot of Angelenos didn't think him saying that was enough to explain it away. Under Gates, the LAPD had cracked down hard on crime, but blacks and Hispanics said they felt harassed by the police. This didn't help police relations with minority communities. To me it didn't look like Gates had done much to get to the bottom of what the minorities were claiming. He wasn't one to put his officers on a leash, and the racial tension around L.A. kept growing.

The members of the Christopher Commission weren't the only ones who concluded it was best for Gates to step down. There were many others who wanted the chief out of office, including conservative writer George F. Will. At this point,

Bradley was all for cleaning house, and he insisted that the LAPD make public the computer messages that appeared racist by the cops who beat me.

Bradley also set up a police commission to look into the LAPD. The commission had five people on it, including Stanley Sheinbaum, who was a board member of the ACLU, which fights for civil rights. Bradley told the commission to look at the LAPD's policies and actions, and he really wanted them to investigate at how the police handled minorities. At the commission's first public hearing, more than four hundred people showed up. A lot of those folks demanded that Gates step down from his post. "There is a very serious crisis in leadership," noted Commissioner Daniel Garcia.

But the boys in blue had each other's backs and the LAPD officers proved to be loyal to their chief. They stuck behind Gates and supported how he ran the department. Mayor Bradley, however, eventually announced that getting rid of Gates was "the only way" for the LAPD to get back on the right track. Gates tried hard to hold on to his job as the head of the police, but he wasn't able to in the end. He gave in and resigned in June 1992, fifteen months after the beating. His fourteen years as chief of police of the LAPD were over, sadly coming to an end under pressure from the Mayor.

CIVIL RIGHTS

Powell, Koon, Wind, and Briseno were indicted for felony assault back in March 1991. That wasn't the only legal case having to do with the beating that year. On May 8, 1991, my wife, Crystal, and I filed a federal civil rights lawsuit against the city of Los Angeles. My lawyer at the time, Steven A. Lerman, wanted my compensation from the city to total $56 million, which would come out to $1 million for each time I got hit by the cops' batons. We eventually decided on asking the city for a much smaller number—$9.5 million—in compensation.

In June 1992, Lerman and I felt good about settling with the city. We drove around town one day, and the papers made a big deal about the car being fancy enough to have its own phone. We needed the phone because we were waiting for a call to tell us when to show up at City Hall. I told the *Los Angeles Times,* "I want to get on with my life. It's great, it's fine if we can get this over with. I want to put the pressure behind me and try to live a normal life." I told the reporter that if I was awarded the money, "I would thank them for working as fast as they could and for getting this thing resolved. And I would thank them for showing some genuine concern."

U.S. District Judge Harry Hupp had issued a gag order, so the City Council wasn't allowed to discuss its deliberations openly. There was talk from City Hall that the council wanted to reach a settlement because they didn't want to risk a repeat of the riots that happened after the not-guilty verdict back in April 1992 for the four officers in the state's case, and they didn't want to drag out the legal stuff surrounding the beating. What they wanted was to rebuild the city after all the violence.

A city official said, "There was some concern of what the city risks if the settlement talks fail and the trial goes ahead. Could the daily exposure to the testimony result in more violence? There were several [council] members who were concerned about that."

Violence wasn't the only thing they were concerned about. They didn't want another round of riots, but they didn't want to end up giving me too much money either. "The council is caught between two different responsibilities. The first is to keep the peace and the other is to minimize the financial burden on the city. The two goals may be in conflict," an official said.

The city wasn't going to just hand over the money Lerman and I had filed suit asking for. My attorney felt they were thinking more along the lines of $5 to $8 million, which was less than what we wanted but could still have been the biggest payment ever made by L.A. to settle a police brutality case. The city had no intention of giving me the money all at once. There was talk of giving me a chunk of the payment up front then paying me the rest in a designated amount every year for the rest of my life.

I have always wondered if the City Council was afraid that if they were to pay me a $5 to $8 million settlement, that payout would only add to the city's worsening financial problems. L.A. was strapped for money and made no secret about it, and if they settled with me for that amount, they were worried it would make them seem like they had more money than they did, or that they wanted everyone to think that they did. Things weren't going their way when it came to L.A. getting its share of the state's budget, and I'm sure they were worried this would just make things worse.

I was open to settling out of court, because it would've meant money in my pocket and no guessing games about what the jury would decide in this case. A jury had already declared the four officers not guilty in the state criminal case, even with that shocking videotape as evidence in court. It was possible that if my lawsuit against the city went to trial, the jury could have sympathy for the other side again instead of me. So I went with what Lerman said: "Today's dollars are worth more than tomorrow's speculation."

The city wasn't able to decide on a settlement the day I was riding around town with Lerman waiting for the call from City Hall, but they eventually decided to offer me $1.25 million to settle out of court. They also accepted that they were liable for the beating. I didn't agree with the amount they were offering, it just felt low to me, and not at all a just amount, so it was back to court.

CIVIL RIGHTS

My civil rights suit against L.A. went to trial in 1994 with U.S. District Judge John G. Davies presiding. Testimonies were heard for three weeks. I switched lawyers and had Milton

Grimes represent me instead of Lerman. We tried to show that the beating was an outright racist attack and that I would never be the same after. My body was damaged, and there were times I would get headaches that left me completely incapacitated. During these attacks I became afraid that I couldn't lead a normal life anymore.

I was excited when told I would take the stand this time. In case you're wondering, by the way, the jury was a mix of races in this trial, and most of the jurors were women. I didn't get the chance during the state trial against the officers, but I would speak for myself now. I finally got to tell the court my side of the story about the beating. I told them that I heard the cops say racist things to me that night while I got it all out, straight and true. I admitted to jury that, yes, I had been drunk that night while I was driving, and when the police started chasing me, I didn't know exactly what I was thinking but believed I panicked.

I was on parole at the time for the grocery-store robbery conviction, and jail was not a place I wanted to go back to. The police testified that I made the cops chase me for a long time, but I told the court that I only tried to run from them for twelve blocks or so after getting off the highway and calling it quits. I knew I couldn't keep running. When the cops surrounded me, I did what they told me to do, but then one of them started taunting me with the line, "How do you feel?" and another called me racist names and told me I better run if

I wanted to stay alive. I was terrified, and when I desperately tried to stand up and get away from them, they started beating me. I told the court, "I was just so scared. I felt like I was going to die." My lawyers pointed out that excessive roughness was routine for the LAPD when it came to dealing with minorities.

My lawyers had taken the audio from the video of my beating and did something to filter out the background noise so that you could hear what the officers were saying. They played the audio in court, and you could hear one of the officers saying, "Nigger, hands behind your back." Judge Davies dismissed this as evidence, though. He said the technology that was used on the audio hadn't been tested enough to make sure you could trust it to be accurate. That was a tough break for me, because even to this day, there is a lingering controversy over whether the N word was uttered that night, but the God-honest truth is that it was.

The racial slurs became a big part of our case. "Rodney King was beaten because of his race," Grimes said in his closing argument. Quite simply, my lawyers told the jury the cops beat me because I'm black. They compared me to civil rights leaders, including Martin Luther King Jr. and Malcolm X. But no way I was holding myself up as an equal to those guys. Never.

I was just a guy who suffered crippling injuries and severely debilitating headaches who was terrified most of the time. I was scared of the police and had become afraid of being outside. Witnesses came into the courtroom and said so. This was a tragedy for me because I really loved being outdoors.

I testified that "I felt like I had been raped. . . . I felt like a cow that was waiting to be slaughtered, like a piece of meat." And that feeling didn't go away when the cops were done beating me. I felt like a moving target. I lived in fear, my lawyers said that I often walked around in a bulletproof vest and surrounded myself with security guards.

But I didn't want to spend my life hiding in fear and was honestly trying to be a better person after my ordeal. I was working on getting my high school diploma, and I was taking quality time to be with my wife and kids. I can't deny it was hard trying to make my life any better at this time. I owed almost $200,000 in medical bills for my injuries, and my head was all messed up. I was dizzy, my eyesight was blurry, my face was numb, and I kept getting flashbacks because of the beating.

The city's lawyers went after me in the trial. They dug into my past and did their best to make me look like an alcoholic and a criminal. They said I was no good in school and I caused a lot of trouble when I was a kid. The city accepted it was liable for my beating, but they didn't accept that the beating was a racist attack. They said the case was just a tort claim—meaning a lawsuit that allowed people to sue the government for wrongful acts by government agencies or their employees. So they took responsibility for the cops beating me, but they said there was no racist motive for what happened. On top of that, the city's lawyers said my injuries weren't as bad as they seemed and my money troubles were my own fault, even though my injuries made it hard to work and make money to support me and my family.

In its closing argument, the city offered to pay me $800,000 for my injuries. This number was way smaller than what I had asked for because they downplayed my injuries to the jury. In Grimes's closing argument, he dropped the $9.5 million we asked the city for back when they were still thinking of a settlement and he asked the jury for $15 million in compensation instead. Grimes told the court I wasn't going to be able to work again because of the beating, and the jury took that into consideration when they decided on what the city owed me in damages. I had been in the construction business at the time of the beating (although I didn't presently have a job), and Grimes said my injuries amounted to me losing wages of around $500,000 to $1 million throughout the rest of my life. My legal team also pointed out that the beating left me with deeply imbedded psychological troubles and post-traumatic stress disorder.

FINAL AWARD

Because the city of L.A. had already accepted it was liable for the beating, the jury only had to decide what to award me based on my injuries and how I would continue to suffer as a result of the beating. After deliberating for close to four days, the jury decided on much less than what Grimes asked for on my behalf, but it was more than what the city wanted to pay. The final award was for $3,816,535.45.

I wasn't there when the jury read the verdict, and I didn't make any comments to the public. Grimes called me to tell me about the award, and I told him I was okay with what they decided. He spoke publicly about our conversation and told people I was "somewhat pleased" with the jury's decision. "He was expecting more, but he has no disagreement with the jury's verdict," Grimes said about me. He also said he told me, "We have not finished. He understood that. The case is not over." Grimes thought I deserved more money.

L.A. City Attorney James Hahn wasn't completely satisfied with the verdict either, but he was okay with it. He said, "We think that the verdict, although higher than the city's last official offer . . . is a satisfactory result. . . . When you make both sides a little unhappy, the jury has done its job." Councilwoman Rita Walters said, "I think it's time that the city put this to rest." But she also said about the $3.8 million that: "As far as I'm concerned, the amount does not compensate for the harm to Mr. King."

The money the jury awarded was meant to compensate me for my medical bills, psychological pain, and loss of income throughout the rest of my life as a direct result of my injuries from the beating. The amount of the award may sound like a big number, but it really didn't chalk up to much for me because on top of my medical bills, I owed Grimes a lot of money, and I also owed my old lawyer Lerman several hundred thousand.

I didn't get the $3.8 million right away. The L.A. City Council approved a plan that held aside at least $2 million. My lawyer requested that this money be divided in half and placed into two funds that two separate annuity companies would manage. These two funds were meant to provide a steady income for me over time. The council agreed, and Councilman Zev Yaroslavsky said, "This is a sound and prudent way to apportion that money. It's got everybody's agreement." Once the $2 million was set aside in those funds, I had $1.8 million left, but again, that's not much, and was more like money already spent when you consider what I already owed in medical bills, and considerable amounts to lawyers and investigators on the case.

The compensation the jury awarded me was clearly much less than Grimes thought I deserved, and when he heard the decision, he said he was "still optimistic we'll reach the $15 million figure" that he had asked the jury for in his closing argument. He was hoping to reach that $15 million during the second part of the trial, which would determine whether the LAPD officers involved in the beating were required to pay punitive damages to me. Grimes was looking at the possibility of a much higher award because earlier lawsuits against the police involving brutality cases had resulted in punitive damages that were up to five times more than compensatory damages, which was what the first part of the trial was about.

There were originally supposed to be more than ten defendants in the second part of the trial, in which the jury would decide on punitive damages. The defendants included Powell, Koon, Wind, Briseno, and former Chief of Police Gates. My lawyers pointed out evidence in the Christopher Commission report that showed Gates to be largely the cause of racist attitudes and behaviors among his officers. But Judge Davies didn't accept the argument against Chief Gates for his accountability in the beating. "Bad management is not enough. Allowing racism is not enough. Poor supervision is not enough," Davies said. He decided to dismiss Gates as a defendant.

Gates was the big fish in this lawsuit, and without him on trial, we were left with the "little fish," as one of my lawyers put it. Koon was now the biggest target among the final group of defendants because he was the highest-ranking officer. But we weren't going to get much from him, seeing as how he was already in prison and, unlike Gates, didn't have much money to begin with.

The final number of defendants was whittled down to seven: Koon, Powell, Wind, Briseno, and fellow cops Rolando Solano and Louis Turriaga, who were also there at the scene the night of the beating. I accused Turriaga of stepping on me when he tried to handcuff me, and I accused him and Solano of being too rough when they dragged me across the asphalt to get me off the road. The seventh defendant was me because Briseno fought me back with a countersuit, claiming I had attacked him before my beating was recorded on video.

It was the jury's job to decide whether the cops had used excessive force and/or violated my civil rights. They also had to decide whether to punish the officers by making them pay me damages. Koon, who was serving his sentence after being convicted in the federal case, appeared in court in his blue prison uniform. Although he had wanted to switch into a suit for the trial, he was not allowed by the warden.

Koon defended his actions, saying he Tasered me and told the other cops to hit me with their batons because he thought I was on drugs and that I resisted arrest. Koon called me "a wily, black ex-convict." He said, "I know I didn't do anything wrong. I acted in good faith. I've taken full responsibility and accountability for my actions."

Powell, who was also serving his prison sentence after conviction in the federal case, said he beat me with his baton because he thought I was dangerous. He also said he did it because Koon, the highest ranking officer on the scene, told him to do it. Like Koon, Powell insisted that he didn't do anything wrong that night. He told the court, "I not only don't think it, I know it." I wasn't sure if it was arrogance, or a blind almost irrational interpretation of their duties, but it just struck me that these guys were living on a different planet when they said that they did nothing wrong to me.

Powell backed up what Koon said about me resisting arrest. "I almost had to shoot him. I could not keep him on the ground," he said. He didn't remember if he hit my head, but he said he went after my arms and legs to make sure I couldn't get away. He thought I would hurt him, and he said he feared for his life. Regarding the fates of the other officers, he said, "I wasn't going to be another statistic. I've stood at enough gravesides and heard 'Amazing Grace' played on the bagpipes from a distant hillside, and it was not going to happen to me."

In his closing argument, Michael Stone, Powell's lawyer, told the jury that Powell acted in fear for his safety that night and that "makes him human." He said, "These are not robocops. They feel fear, and they react, and even if he overreacts, if it's an overreaction to an honest fear, who would blame him?"

At least Briseno realized the cops had all gone beyond the call of duty. He tried to separate himself, yet again, from the other officers. "I look over at Larry and Stacey and I think, 'Is it only me that's admitted something wrong happened out there?'" he said to the court about the beating. Briseno said he didn't agree with what Powell did. He thought it wasn't right for Powell to keep hitting me when I was already down on the ground. It looked to him like Powell had lost control. "When I looked at Officer Powell, I saw a frightened man," he said. "He was scared. I don't know if you'd call it a trance. I saw his eyes as wide as they could possibly be. I'd never seen that look before."

I could not help having some feelings for Briseno's position. You could tell he was having a really tough time. He looked very thin, and it was obvious he couldn't stand having become an outcast to the police as a result of being the only one who showed regret for the beating. "For three years, I've put up with this and it hurts," he said. "Look around this courtroom at these officers. Not one of them likes me. No one across the street [at LAPD HQ] likes me."

The lawyers of the cops argued against them having to pay me damages because they said the cops had also suffered because of the beating and they had no money to give me. They said their careers were ruined and they no longer had any savings. They said they even lost their homes. Wind's wife took the stand and started crying when she told the court about what a hard time her family was having. Koon's lawyer, Ira Salzman, said, "The officers have been victimized just like Rodney King."

REACTION TO VERDICT

When it came time to deliberate, the jury took eleven days and reached the verdict that Koon and Powell acted with malice during the beating. But they also decided that the officers on trial had suffered enough and did not need to pay me anything in damages. As for Briseno's countersuit, the jury decided that I was guilty of shoving Briseno in the chest before the beating, but they decided that I didn't act out of malice and I did not have to pay him damages.

The jury's decision was unanimous, but it wasn't reached without a lot of back and forth. There were some bad feelings left. One juror, a seamstress from South Pasadena, said to reporters, "There was no justice here . . . no justice at all. It's purely black and white."

I wasn't there when they announced the verdict, and I didn't comment. Grimes spoke out: "How do you give a man $3,816,535.45 who was beaten and not consider the badness of the beaters?" He said the jury "didn't take the opportunity to put an exclamation point at the end of this case, to let those officers know that if they beat someone they face punitive damages."

Councilwoman Rita Walters said, "It seems to me the purpose of punitive damages is to extract a level of responsibility from someone who perpetrated an act that was harmful to someone else." So she thought the jury's decision not to require the officers to pay me damages was "beyond the realm of understanding."

Koon's lawyer, Salzman, was pleased with the verdict. He said the police "can now do their job and not fear this vindictive prosecution."

Wind was the only one of the cops on trial that was in court the day of the verdict. He told reporters, "This has been a long road I've traveled and I am very pleased with the decision." The guy ended up pretty broke and was jobless after the whole mess. "It's taken a chunk out of my life, a big chunk," he said.

Grimes wasn't satisfied with the verdict, so he filed for appeals. One appeal was for the verdict that the city did not owe me punitive damages (the $3.8 million the city was ruled to pay me in the first phase of the trial was for compensatory damages). The second appeal was for the verdict that Briseno was not guilty of battering me so he did not owe me punitive damages. Grimes eventually withdrew the appeals and made an agreement with the city and Briseno. The city stopped coming after me to pay $28,600 worth of their legal bills, and Briseno stopped demanding I pay him $3,400 for his legal fees. Grimes told people I wanted to move on with my life: "He wishes to really put this behind him."

RIOTS QUIET

As for the rest of the city, there was no rioting this time around. Fletcher Jordan, a guy who works at a sporting goods store in Baldwin Hills, was quoted in the *Los Angeles Times,* "I'm really glad this is over. It's been a long process that we've been going through. Everyone."

But just because the city was quiet after this verdict didn't mean everyone felt justice had been done. A UCLA student in South Central, Trina White, told the *Times* she didn't like the verdict: "once again, the police are getting off scot-free," she said. She was also upset that the city's taxpayers, instead of the cops involved, now had the burden of paying me damages.

John Mack, who was the Urban League's president back then, didn't like the jury's decision that Koon and Powell didn't have to pay me anything. "True, they are serving time, but they are doing so without showing any contrition," he said. "You can't run around brutalizing every African American young man that you encounter."

Police officers felt badly for the cops that stood trial and for the LAPD getting a bad rap as a whole after the beating. Jeff Hart, an officer in the LAPD's Foothill Division, where I was chased down by the cops the night of the beating, said, "Those police officers did what they had to do to go home safe that night, and the citizens and the media destroyed this department for it." Sergeant Leonard Ross, a black man who represented other black cops as president of the Oscar Joel Bryant Association, also sided with his fellow cops. He said that I "got paid" while the cops "are in prison. This trial was just like shooting a dead person."

Publicly I said that I wanted to leave this whole thing behind. "I would like it to end," I told people. "No one wins here in this type of situation." And I meant that, but it seemed the cops had gotten off lightly.

At the time I believed that it would never really be over. As Wind said, "It's the [Rodney] King case. It's never over with. It's made a wreck of our lives, a wreck of the city and of our profession." But now, twenty years later, I disagree. I feel I've worked hard to heal physically and spiritually and I've been able to move on in a lot of ways. And I hope and want to believe that L.A. is more tolerant and promising than ever. Things only stayed wrecked if you don't make an effort to fix them.

MORE TROUBLE

I wish I could say the beating and the court trials that came after were the last of my troubles with the law, but they weren't.

I wish I could go back and have a talk with that restless, broken Rodney and tell him to grow up, get sober, and chill the hell out. But I can't.

On May 11, 1991, a couple months after the beating, I was pulled over in Santa Fe Springs because the cops said I had illegally tinted windows. I didn't have my license on me, and my registration had expired, but they didn't cite me. On May 28, I was arrested for something else. A vice officer said he caught me with a hooker in Hollywood. What made it worse is that the officer said he found me with a transvestite and that I tried to run the officer over with my car. I admit trying to blow by him, but I only did that because I didn't know he was a cop and I thought he was trying to rob me. I was released without being charged.

On July 16, 1992, the cops arrested me again for drunk driving, but they didn't file any charges. My lawyer explained that I was probably drinking a lot because I was so stressed out from the beating. Later, he said the cops arrested me because I'm black.

On August 21, 1993, I crashed my car into a block wall in downtown L.A. Tests showed I had two times the legal limit of alcohol in my blood. I pleaded no contest and was convicted of DUI. I know I was in a lot of pain all the time, and was drinking to dull some of it, but that's no excuse. I volunteered to enter an alcohol rehab program for sixty days. I had to pay a $1,438 fine and do community service for twenty days. I also got three more years of probation.

In May 1995, I was arrested and charged with DUI again,

this time in Pennsylvania. I was in Union Township for the funeral of my father-in-law, and I was riding around on a country road when the car ran off the road. It was late at night, and the police said they smelled alcohol on me. The police also said I would not take a blood alcohol test. When the case went to trial, Sean Thompson, who's distantly related to me, testified that he was driving, not me. He said I was only a passenger and that the car was a rental. The jury took almost seven hours to deliberate. If they had found me guilty, I would've gone back to jail for sixty days in Pennsylvania and possibly six more months on top of that back in L.A. because of my earlier DUI conviction. Luckily, the jury acquitted me.

In addition to the DUIs, there were accusations of spousal abuse. On June 26, 1992, Crystal told the police I hit her when we were fighting, and the cops arrested me. Crystal didn't file a complaint, though, and there were no charges against me. That wasn't the last of the domestic dispute stuff. On the evening of July 14, 1995, Crystal and I were returning from a day trip in our Ford Explorer. We started fighting, so I pulled off the road. We kept arguing, and at one point she got out of the car. As she was smoking a cigarette I guess we had gotten so loud that Gina Amador, a woman who lived in one of the surrounding houses, called 911 and told the operator: "He ran her over! He ran her over! He ran her over!"

The police came and arrested me. I was accused of domestic violence and assault with a deadly weapon (the car). They said Crystal had been forced out of the car and that I drove off. The truth was when she tried to reach back in to get her purse, which she had left on the passenger seat, she got dragged along with the moving car before falling and hitting the ground. She had to get seven stitches for a cut on her forehead and I spent the night in jail.

The case went to trial. Crystal filed a statement that said we "were arguing and he made me get out of the car. I reached in the car to get my wallet. Can't remember if the car was moving but he drove off with me on it." In court, she testified that she had reached in through the window on my side of the car and tried to get her wallet and that I said to her, "You better get off the car."

I told the court, "I was just trying to get out of there. I didn't care—I mean I did care if she was OK, but I'd seen that she was OK. She was getting up. I didn't try to do nothing to hurt her. But it gave me a bad rap. It messed me up. That hurt me more than anything that I ever did."

And it did. I was depressed for months. The jury found me guilty of a misdemeanor hit-and-run. The sentence was ninety days in jail, and I served twenty days in L.A. County jail. But the jury acquitted me of the charges of assault with a deadly weapon, reckless driving, and spousal abuse. Unfortunately, Crystal filed for divorce.

There was another purse-related incident soon after the unfortunate occurrence with Crystal. On the evening of July 21, 1995, a man ran to a cop car and said, "I just saw a young black man running down Brand Boulevard with a lady's purse," and he pointed me out. This was in downtown Glendale. I told the cop I wasn't stealing anything. I said the purse was mine and that I did not run away from a crowd. What I was doing was rushing to get to L.A. Cellular so I could pay my pager bill before the place closed. What I was holding was my own leather pouch. The police said I was nervous and upset. The cop frisked me and looked through my car. The "purse" was on my front seat, and the cop figured out that it belonged to me, so I hadn't committed a crime.

Steve Lerman, who was back to being my lawyer again, thought the whole thing might have been a bad joke played by the guy who accused me of stealing. The cop didn't try to find out if someone had actually lost a purse before stopping and questioning me. Lerman said, "It's the old story. A white guy runs out of a store and he is jogging. A black guy runs out of a store and he is a thief."

My run-ins with the police just kept going. There were nice periods of less pain, less headaches, and relative calm but then I'd have a bad couple of nights, start hitting the 40s and everything would crumble. In 1999, they accused me of hurting my sixteen-year-old daughter, Candance, and her mom, Carmen Simpson. They came to my house the night of January 31 but didn't arrest me. Carmen said Candance went to the hospital after we fought. On March 3, the cops issued a warrant on me for spousal battery, child abuse, and vandalism. I turned myself in and got a sentence of ninety days in jail in San Bernardino County. I was also required to go to treatment programs for battery and child abuse.

I was involved in more incidents the next decade. In September 2001, the cops arrested me in Pomona for indecent exposure and for being on PCP. I had to attend a drug treatment program for a year. In April 2003, I drove my Ford Expedition into a fence in San Bernardino at 100 mph. I pleaded guilty to being on PCP and had to go to drug rehab for six months. I also got a sentence of 120 days in jail. In October 2003, I was arrested in Rialto because the cops suspected me of punching my girlfriend in the stomach. The police didn't prosecute. In September 2005, the cops arrested me because I supposedly threatened to kill my daughter and her mom when they were arguing with my then girlfriend. The police didn't prosecute that case either.

As recently as July 2011, I was arrested for drunk driving in Moreno Valley. In August, I was charged with DUI. The cops said I was drunk past the legal limit and high on marijuana. I pleaded not guilty in November because I believed I was under the limit. If convicted, I could get a year in jail.

The only pattern here is that I seem unable to break the pattern. Alcohol acts as the trigger to most of my run-ins with the law, yet I always seem to relapse because alcohol tones down the stress, puts me in a better mood, and dulls the still-very-present and persistent pain. I know that's no excuse, but it seems to resurface as such again and again.

RELAPSE—REHAB

I was so proud of the work I did with Dr. Drew and his rehab program that I've devoted all of Chapter 8 to my time on VH1's shows *Celebrity Rehab* and *Sober Living*. But despite all the work I put into getting better, and enjoying over a year of being clean and sober, I fell off the damn wagon again. In AA and other programs, they say that with some recovering alcoholics, relapsing can be a necessary step in achieving permanent sobriety. But I doubt they mean as often as I have.

The fact that my father was a hopeless alcoholic and that I've obviously picked up DD (Dad's Disease) is no excuse for me. I do wish that my father didn't drink himself to death at the age of forty-two. I do think I would've had a better chance at staying away from the bottle myself and might have avoided a lot of the problems I've written down in this chapter. I've felt unfortunate learning about the stats regarding children of alcoholics, and how the deck has been stacked against me. I have been ashamed with my behavior countless times over the years, but I must believe I have the power to put an end to this self-destructive pattern.

Dr. Drew and other experts that work with addicts taught me about positive reinforcement, remembering the times being sober was a positive part of my life. I look back on the clarity and power I had when I'm sober, like when I made that speech to the people of Los Angeles, and I'm determined to build on it. Staying busy with my daily life is a big part of it, and this book is part of that effort. Becoming engaged to an intelligent, supportive woman like Cynthia is also extremely helpful.

I also want to become more active with my grandchild, my

daughters, and the other members of my family. But it's difficult at times because I get depressed when I'm dealing with constant stiffness in my joints and severe headaches. I know a drink will allow me to feel better instantly, and that's a powerful temptation I absolutely must resist.

Chapter 6

CHOOSE OR LOSE

RODNEY ROULETTE

Have you ever gotten so close to a person that you feel like he could be your brother from another mother? You go through tough times with people like that, and they stick by you, they believe in you. They tell you it's all going to be fine because they've got your back. You just have to hang tough and soldier through.

These people you trust during trying times might be doctors, lawyers, preacher men, or teacher men. But no matter, because whether you're up against cops or cancer, you feel blessed. They are in your corner for all fifteen rounds. That was what I looking for in a lawyer. I was fortunate to have influential people—everyone from Al Sharpton and Johnnie Cochran to Mayor Bradley and President George Bush—reach out to me with advice and encouragement. But when I asked a few of them about hiring lawyers, they were clear that the final decision had to be mine. Well, that is where I go from being truly blessed to completely cursed. I am the all-time worst judge of character and capabilities. Like a child, I am easily impressed and more easily duped, mainly because I want to believe, I want to follow. And I just couldn't pick a clear winner when it came to legal representation.

I talked to dozens of attorneys, and didn't know which ones were worse, the ones I worked with or the ones who wanted to work with me. An attorney I spoke with assured me he would keep me flush with booze and pot while he represented me. One lawyer told me that he could make all my legal problems go away if I would just buy him a Bentley. I didn't know how to react. He wanted me to have that $100,000 car sitting in the driveway of his home by the end of the week. I honestly thought he was kidding and went along with the joke. I said, "You sure I can't just buy you a Rolls? It's the same company." No, he responded, it had to be a Bentley. It wasn't until then that I realized he wasn't fooling around. Believe me, this was just the beginning of the craziness.

In 1991, when I began the process of hiring my first lawyer, I was hardly recovered from the trauma of that spring. My body was still weak and broken, and my mind was, too. Looking back, it's no wonder I made mistakes with lawyers and lawsuits.

But I tried to start at the right place. I went to the one person I knew I could trust, and that was my mother. I was delighted when she said that she had a suggestion for an attorney. After the beating, Warren Wilson, a respected journalist who was with KTLA for over twenty years, sat with Mom and had an open, honest conversation with her about what we could expect and what we should prepare for. When he stood to leave, he handed my mother a card with an attorney's name and contact information. I took the card from Mom and called the name on it: Steven Lerman. After my conversation with Lerman, and then after thinking about what he said, I knew I could trust him. It felt right on a gut level.

And so I looked to Lerman to help me through the civil suit against the city of Los Angeles, and my efforts to get monetary compensation for my injuries after the criminal trial that found the officers not guilty. I couldn't work. And I had no idea how long it would be before I could work again. The headaches were nearly constant, and my knee was still giving me trouble. I was a mess, physically and psychologically, and the beating was in my head day in and day out. I didn't know what was going to become of me, and I was afraid things would be really difficult for my family if we didn't win a civil suit for enough money to take care of us.

But the first time I heard about any kind of payout for my injuries, it did not come from any attorney; it came from the mayor himself. I received a call directly from Mayor Bradley. He was friendly and warm, and knew to call me my middle name, Glen. Well, the mayor said he had thought long and hard over the hardships I had suffered and wanted to make it up to me.

Mayor Bradley offered to send me to a four-year college, pay the tuition for any institution of my choice, *and* pay me $200,000 in cash. I listened carefully to the mayor, who sounded completely sincere. There was no trace of urgency or manipulation in his voice. I believed he was not trying to pull a fast one on me. I was very tempted to just say, "Yes sir. Let's do it!" But something made me tell him I would need to think about it.

To this day I think Mayor Bradley believed he was reaching out to try to resolve a potentially difficult situation in a constructive way. I even admired the way he considered my education as a priority in his offer. I remember right at the end of the conversation, his voice quavered a little bit. "Well, you think about it, Glen, but please get back to me as soon as you can." I thanked him and hung up. I think he really wanted the whole thing to go away, because he had been mayor for like a quarter century and the last thing he needed was anything like this putting a black mark on his career right at the end of his run.

Some people close to me have called it an attempted bribe, and others a settlement offer. Steve Lerman just told me to grab it. "That's a good amount, Glen. I'd take it." I won't lie, it was a good amount. And I was tempted to take it and try to put the whole thing behind me. But I knew my medical bills, and how long I'd been out of work since the beating, and how afraid I was about the future and taking care of my family. And Lerman knew those things, too. He knew how I felt and what I was afraid of, and why I needed to file suit against the city, and why I needed to win. So that he was so quick to tell me to take it made me suspect for the first time that maybe I had the wrong attorney. Things only got worse with Lerman after that. He was in over his head, and his wanting to take the first offer of money was just a warning.

Unfortunately, as much as I like him personally, Lerman was primarily a personal injury attorney, and that was not the ideal qualification for the type of counsel I needed. Soon, I'd have to find another man to lean on, and I think Lerman knew that day was coming before I did. Lerman himself told the press that representing me was like being married to a beautiful woman. He said that meant as soon as the husband left the room, every guy was coming over to chat the beautiful girl up. I thought that was pretty funny, and damn close to the truth too. It seemed like every lawyer in L.A. called to tell me how their experience and strategy was better than my present representation.

THE CIRCUS BEGINS

Shortly after I first hired Lerman in 1991, I was repeatedly warned by other attorneys about his lack of experience with my sort of case, and soon began to get really concerned that I'd made the wrong decision because Lerman was primarily a personal injury attorney.

Everything was riding on our suits against the city. I began taking calls from other attorneys who came right out and said it: "Steve Lerman is borderline incompetent in this area of the law." They said I would suffer the consequences if I did not do something right away. Granted, it was just the opinions of other lawyers who probably wanted my business, but, I admit, it scared me. What could I do to take care of myself and my family, and to find some kind of justice?

As my faith in Lerman's abilities faded, I started fishing around for another attorney.

I remember early on in the process, before I started with Steve Lerman, I got one of those attorney proposals in the mail from his office. This was before the O.J. trial shot him to international fame. In it was a list of his accomplishments, a glossy photo, and a nice letter from him, addressed to me and personally signed. I remembered one of the first things Lerman had done was call Johnnie Cochran to ask what I should settle on. Johnny said nothing less than a "cool million." Cool Cochran.

Two years later, when I was openly casting around for other attorneys, Johnny Cochran and I finally met. I was excited. The O. J. Simpson trial hadn't yet happened, but Cochran was already big and famous by then because of the Michael Jackson case, and a part of me thought this might be my grand solution. Cool Cochran on my side! Can you imagine if I had gone with Cochran? *The way he was hit, you must not acquit!*"

He ranted about the horrors I had endured from both sides, and how he could finally, personally, make sure that justice was done. Then he flashed that Cool Cochran smile and leaned back in his chair.

"You need to know something," he said. "I don't need you."

He absolutely did not need to represent me for publicity purposes, that was true. I wasn't sure he was making big money off the Michael Jackson case, but I guess it didn't matter. Johnny said he'd be glad to head up my legal team, with one demand.

He looked at me like he was God Almighty and said, by the way, that his rate was half the total take. His exact words: "Fifty percent. Take it or leave it."

Well, that was one time I didn't have to think it over. Despite my hopes that he'd be the one to lead my charge, I had to tell him right then and there: "No thanks, Mr. Cochran. But I appreciate your time anyway, and let's stay in touch."

No sense in burning any bridges. Cochran kind of blinked, and offered a weak-ass smile. I think his ego had him convinced I was going to jump at the chance to have him as my attorney. But it seemed to me that with Cochran, it was only about the money.

WORKING TOWARD A WIN

Finally, I turned to my wife, Crystal, for advice. Crystal's family was from Newcastle, Pennsylvania, and her aunt was friends with Al Barnes, who played for the Detroit Lions in the 1970s and knew a lot of powerful people. After about a week of back and forth, Crystal's aunt recommended I reach out to an attorney named Milton Grimes, who was big in criminal defense law. He had a reputation as a bulldog, a tough courtroom attorney who simply got the job done.

So after a year and a half of working with Steve Lerman, I jumped. I signed up with Milton Grimes and told Lerman I had to do what was right for me and my family. But by then civil suits had already been filed against the city, and by the time Grimes replaced Lerman, I was waist deep in those—

and civil suits weren't Grime's specialty! But I was not going to consider switching again, although the damn phone never stopped ringing during those days with referrals.

Well, Grimes started fast. We agreed on his 25 percent cut, just as I had with Lerman. And he got to work building a team, a big one. He ended up employing fourteen other lawyers to help him with my case. Pile in, boys, the gravy train is leaving the station and you'll want to hop on board. As his main co-counsels, Grimes brought in a medical specialist, a guy named Federico Castelan Sayre, from Newport Beach; and for a civil rights specialist, he got John Burris from Oakland.

He also started taking care of me personally. Very quickly, I grew to respect and trust this man, and his loving wife, Eloise. They treated me as an equal, and welcomed me as a special guest in their home. In Eloise I saw a compassionate, intelligent woman who was deeply shaken when she viewed the video of my beating. We can learn a lot about a man by the woman who chooses to stand by his side, and Eloise raised my opinion of Milton Grimes. I could honestly say that I grew close to both of them.

He also started advancing me a fair amount of money, to take care of bills and living expenses while we moved forward with our suit against the city. Somewhere there were court files that showed Grimes had advanced me a fair amount that year, starting in late 1991. In fact, the figure was over $100,000. (Lerman chimed in around the same time and said he'd given over $150,000 prior to my switching to Grimes, though that figure seemed high.)

And Grimes came through. He was a master in the court-room. He asked for more than $9 million in damages at the beginning, but that last day in court, he looked right at the jury and told them after thinking about it all, and seeing all this evidence, he thought it ought to be $15 million.

I wasn't in the courtroom the day the decision came down. I'd spent the last three years fighting for justice, and had been told several times that there was going to be an announcement, and then nothing happened. I never imagined it would take so long to settle the suits. But finally, when it all ended, the jury told the city of Los Angeles to pay me just over $3.8 million in damages. I was pleased, or as pleased as I could be. It was hard to feel too happy about anything back then. But I remember breathing a sigh of relief, and feeling like maybe I'd done okay after all, maybe I'd take care of my family like I wanted to. Joseph Duff made a statement that took the words right out of my mouth: "It is a measure of the depth of pain and suffer-ing and the understanding that there is a permanent injury to him." Permanent was the right word. But the announcement of that payout lifted a burden.

Three point eight million dollars. I still remember the first time I heard it. Cochran's prediction of a million had been on the low side. And the final total was almost twenty times more than the amount Mayor Bradley had offered me.

On top of it, the federal judge ordered the city to pay me an additional $1.6 million to take care of the attorneys' fees. It wasn't ever about the money for me. But hearing that news made me breathe even easier. The attorneys would be taken care of, and I'd have the award money to take care of my family for the rest of my life and theirs. It had been a rough run for me, but finally I was seeing the light at the end of the tunnel.

Or so I thought.

MONEY MAYHEM

It should have been a happy time, I guess, but the drama didn't end with the jury's award. There were problems I guess I should have seen coming. One big one would haunt me: no one seemed to know who should get the money. To me, it was simple. It was my award, based on the wrong done to me—the injuries that had kept me from working, created huge medical expenses, and would stick with me for the rest of my life. So the money should come to me, and I should pay the attorneys just as we'd agreed at the beginning. But it didn't play out that way. I remember when Maxine Waters, the U.S. representative for California's Twenty-Ninth Congressional District, told me that the city could not send the check directly to me, that it had to go to Lerman or Grimes. Suddenly all the relief I'd felt when the award was announced just disappeared.

One thing I've learned about lawyers—it's never as simple as you think. Turns out, the money wasn't coming to me at all, but to all the attorneys who wanted a piece of the pie. See, neither Lerman nor Grimes specified in their contracts with me who would receive the attorney fees that got awarded to successful plaintiffs in civil rights cases. Lerman and Grimes just didn't know much about civil rights litigation. And their contracts didn't have clauses covering the possibility that these special fees—what they called "statutorily authorized"—might be awarded.

I went over the handling of these fees with three or four lawyers, but the law seemed to be unclear, and nobody knew the answer to how the lawyers should be paid. Through no fault of my own, it was an incredibly confusing mess, and the response I got from most of the law firms I spoke with was: "We'll have to get back to you on that, Mr. King." The law simply did not state whether these fees belonged to the attorneys or the winning plaintiff, which I hoped would be me. But it did say one thing: that the winning plaintiff can use these fees to pay his attorneys. In my civil rights suit, the city must have been just as confused as I was because they made out the checks for the fees jointly to me and to various attorneys.

So Grimes said I should immediately sign over to him the attorney's fees awarded in the names of the other attorneys. He told reporters he did this in an attempt to prevent trouble, that he even tried to get me to sign a supplemental contract assigning any victor's attorneys' fees to these lawyers.

But why was I getting all this from the press and not Grimes? He didn't have an answer for that. All I was hearing was Grimes ordering me around—do this, do that, sign this, and agree to that—but without any explanation. When Grimes started telling me that I had to surrender to him checks with my name on them, I got defensive. But I was learning: "I'll have to get back to you on that, Mr. Grimes."

Then wham! Next thing I knew, Grimes had cut me off from my monthly allowance. I hadn't received any money from the award yet, and no sense of when I would. I'm sure Grimes would say he had a reason for doing it, but I just figured it was proof he was going to try to strong arm me the rest of the way.

It really confused me when Grimes went all militant in his handling of me. As I said, we'd grown close. But when Grimes cut off my allowance, that's when I felt I had no choice but to find somebody who would help me get the money we'd worked so hard for. I had to go back to Lerman. Later I even testified: "I thought that Steve would take care of me." And I really meant that.

The only reason I went back to Steve Lerman was to have him help me get the money that was awarded me, the money that was going to be a fresh start for me and my family, and I'll never forget Lerman's reaction. He sounded downright joyous over the phone, his voice boomed in my ear: "I knew you'd come back to the godfather!" It seemed like a strange comment, but I was intent on trusting Lerman to do what was necessary to secure the money due to me. I knew that Lerman had been found deserving of statutory attorneys' fees by U.S. District Judge John Davies, who presided at the civil rights trial, so I knew there would be plenty of motivation on his part to get all the award money due me.

During this time, I was totally stressed out, wasn't eating, and was barely sleeping. I didn't know where the next rent check was coming from or how I was going to take care of my family. The headaches came back with a vengeance and I was just a wreck.

But when I hung up with "godfather" Lerman, I definitely felt better. I remember telling him, "Man, I just want to be able to breathe again." After months of lawyer hell, I finally felt like I could.

Here was a man that shortly after I hired him the first time, told my mom that she needn't worry, that he would always protect me. That may sound unprofessional and kind of sappy, but it meant a lot to me. It mattered to me that this lawyer had taken the time to sit down with my mother, look her in the eyes, and tell her of his sincere intention to guide me safely through all that was ahead.

Eight years later, Lerman was quoted in the *Los Angeles Daily Journal* saying, "King has really been misguided. I made a promise to his mother a long time ago that I would always take care of her son, and I'm the only one that didn't screw him." I would like to see what Lerman's dictionary says about the word *screw*. He knew how desperate I was, and how I needed somebody with expertise and drive to get me the money. Lerman had me, and he knew it. But I wasn't just going to give up.

Of course the press snapped it all up and had a field day over the legal infighting, making a mockery of my May 1992 L.A. riots speech to "just get along." How did I expect to inspire others to find peace with their fellow man when I couldn't even get along with my attorneys?

The simple fact was that I felt like I had taken so much abuse from the police, abuse I relived in my mind over and over, and now my own legal team was working me over too. Grimes, whose law firm had received checks cut by the City of Los Angeles, simply decided that the $1.6 million awarded by the judge was theirs and theirs alone. I did not receive a nickel from Grimes.

Of course, I had no problem with anyone who represented me getting paid—if they put in the hours, billed out honestly, and contributed to the team. But the greed these attorneys displayed was just unbelievable. They had found a King-size meal ticket, and they were not about to let go under any circumstances. Several of them even went so far as to request reimbursement for the hours they spent being interviewed by the news media and for their appearances on talk shows like *The Oprah Winfrey Show* and *The Phil Donahue Show*.

It just didn't make sense to me. These guys were getting a ton of free exposure and that was no doubt boosting people's awareness of their names, their law firms, and the services they were offering. If they had to go out and pay a firm for the same amount of PR, it would cost a bundle. And even if the interview didn't go smoothly, or ole Phil Donahue said something to pick them apart, there was still no such thing as bad publicity.

Even Grimes got in the act. He wanted to be paid for attending a movie premiere in Oakland, California, of a film based on the life of Malcolm X. This, of course, included all his cabs, the flight from L.A., hotel room, and meals. No wonder Grimes's bill was the largest. He is reported to have billed $2 million in expenses. Lerman is right behind him, with $1.2

in expenses. The civil rights attorney, John Burris, billed for $600,000 total fees, and medical malpractice attorney Federico Sayre's tab came to $600,000 also.

The city wasn't about to be a blank check for these guys. Among the services they challenged were the fees Grimes paid to have me tutored on African-American history and culture. When questioned, Grimes said the history lessons were important in giving me a greater sense of self-worth and helping me gain some self-esteem. Looking back, I would rather have seen that movie about Malcolm X. But at the time, I embraced having a tutor help me with a sense of who I was as a black man in America. I thought it was a good idea to bone up on the teachings of Martin Luther King Jr., Malcolm X, and Medgar Evers. I read about their courage and vision, and it gave me a greater sense of the responsibility that came with the way people perceived me, as a symbol.

Some of the bills submitted by the attorneys must have been duplicates and I believe that was one of the things that finally set U.S. District Judge John G. Davies off. One of the attorneys not involved in the case actually said Davies "kicked some of the lawyers in the butt." They deserved it, because if it was up to them, the city should just pay them as much as they asked for and shut up. Davies ended up awarding John Burris only $325,000 of the $600,000 he was after; and the same amount, $325,000, went to Fred Sayre.

Steve Lerman's fees were set at $221,000, a hell of a lot less than the $1.2 million he was after. Grimes was awarded the largest amount of all, $456,000, although that was a little less than a quarter of the $2 million he'd billed out. I was around these guys for months and months, and I honestly couldn't tell you if they actually thought they were entitled to these large amounts or were just playing some game. Maybe they believed the only way to get any decent amount was to request ridiculously high fees knowing that even if the judge only gave them a fraction of that chunk, it would still be a solid six-figure (or more) total.

Grimes was upset when he found out that Davies flat out turned down any fees for anything having to do with the media. This included his attending that Malcolm X premier in Oakland. And the lawyers who were with me when I went on Oprah and Donahue got zip.

John Burris was the first to bitch openly about Davies's decision. It turns out he was one of the lawyers who did not seek any reimbursement for time spent dealing with the news media or daytime talk shows. But he agreed with the other lawyers that Davies "was ruthless in disallowing hours associated with the media." Burris, however, had a different sore point. He said he wasn't surprised by Davies's rulings but was "dismayed." He called the judge "unkind as it related to any appearance that work was duplicated."

Davies fired back a shot of his own when he said that "Mr. King's lawyers and Mr. Lerman especially basked in the friendly glow of media attention" to promote themselves. "It is inconceivable that the jury verdicts were related even in the remotest fashion to appearances by the lawyers on talk shows or by the media spin of Mr. King's trial lawyers."

I know that Lerman was pretty upset and complained that the media coverage around me was awfully intense and resulted in his having to be on the job 24-7. He claimed that what he billed was just a small amount of the time he had actually spent working. Then he said something that kind of gave me a snapshot of what was going on in his head. He said: "The entire world media looked to me to offer commentary on Rodney King as a person."

That was upsetting to me. I felt he made it sound like I was just a lump of clay who sat in front of journalists and talk show hosts, didn't say a thing, and let Lerman shape who I was. If what he said was true, then Steve Lerman would be well known today for being the Kingmaker, creator of the image of who I was and what I was thinking. And that just ain't the case.

Can you imagine me going home at night and trying to explain the battles for the lawyers' cuts, the media courtship, and all the other noise to my mom and my family? It gave me a headache just trying to keep up with everything, and I was getting pretty severe migraines all the time as it was. One evening we decided not to talk about lawyers at the table, and that was the best meal we had all year.

We didn't have enough of those meals. While the lawyer fights and court dates filled our days, the headaches and nightmares filled the nights, and the rest of the time we were stressed out and worried about how we were going to make it. My marriage was on the rocks. . . .

MALCOLM X

Time has helped me get the perspective I lacked back then when the trials were swirling all around me. It took everything I had just to get through the day, and my drinking didn't do any good at all. I would be dragging some mornings, not wanting to even see a lawyer, feeling like it was all hopeless.

It feels good to finally respond to the confusion all of this infighting caused. I'm sure there're still a lot of people out there that believe I was just a puppet on a string, serving up the needs of politicians and civil rights activists. But I have never tried to be anyone other than me, and although that is often nothing to be proud of, I refuse to be a phony, or to pretend that I'm something I'm not.

There's a story my father told me about a woman who knew Malcolm X when he was growing up. Her name was Mrs. Alcock, and she lived in Malcolm's neighborhood and knew him as a pup. Mrs. Alcock always went to church and was always trying to help people. If she heard someone was sick, she would be sure to take them something.

Mrs. Alcock knew that Malcolm's family was hurting for money and that they had no food. She knew about Malcolm stealing from the local grocer's and the corner fruit stands, and she had witnessed him doing some other unsavory things.

One day she ran into Malcolm on the street, and she said, "Malcolm, there's one thing I like about you. You're no good, but you don't try to hide it. You're not a hypocrite."

That kind of stuck with me over the years. I am nothing special, but I have never tried to hide that, never tried to be someone I wasn't.

A lot of people who were working on the civil cases with me got all wide-eyed when the camera lights snapped on, kind of hyperventilating all over me. They'd smile and nod at anything I'd say and cozy up close to me. I guess they thought they just had to be next to me when I was talking to the press and they'd be next in line for an interview.

I had a PR person tell me that she got a kick out of seeing the suck-ups on TV that jockey to stand behind the mayor or the chief of police when they're making a public statement. She said it happens in politics, finance, and even with entertainers on the red carpet. Anytime anyone is getting their fifteen minutes, there's someone trying to stand on the watch face with them. Once I was aware of it, it was hilarious to watch.

I was never comfortable with reporters and the whole media glare, but I've gotten more used to it over the years. I will never, however, get the hang of dealing with lawyers. It's just not going to happen. One reason for this is because I could not understand all that legal double-talk. I haven't been dealt the best education or IQ, but I will try to keep up in a room. And if someone was patient with me, I would eventually get the gist of whatever legal strategy they were proposing.

I believed Steve Lerman and I had a good relationship. But then something happened that left me really shocked and kind of sad. And it just proved my worst fears about dealing with people who think they're smarter than me and have had the benefit of a college education.

Lerman purchased the same kind of video recorder for me that George Holliday used to record my beating by the LAPD. I was trying to get the hang of using it, but there were a lot of fancy optional functions for bright daylight, sports speed, auto focus, variable lens, and everything. Someone had either forgotten to give me the owner's manual or lost it. So I gave it to one of Lerman's co-workers to see if he could locate the manual or figure out how to record with it properly.

The next day I had to drop by Lerman's office to go over some documents. Before long, it was lunchtime so I went out to grab a burger at In-N-Out. They have the best damn burgers and fries on earth, and with an XL cola, that is one tasty treat.

When I went back to the office, we went over a bunch more documents that I either needed to read or read and sign. Afterwards, I decided to lie down for about a half hour. One of those severe headaches had crept up on me while I was reading, the kind that felt like the top front of my head was going to blow clear off. *Pound, pound, pound,* but with a chisel, not a sledgehammer. I remember this particular one because it was making me awful sick to my stomach, and I wanted my In-N-Out to stay in. So I put my head down.

I must have tried to nod off for a good twenty minutes, but the headache was too much and I knew I just had to get home. As I got up to leave, Lerman's co-worker came out of his cubicle and handed the video camera back to me. He was going to show me something about operating it, but I was feeling too rotten, so I just left with it.

Later on at home, when I was feeling a little better, I began to play around with the video again. Well, Lerman's co-worker must have been messing with it himself back at the office when someone asked him what he was doing with my video camera.

When I hit the play button I heard, God as my witness, a voice saying: ". . . you got to be kidding!" And then the co-worker's voice: "Yeah, he's too damn dumb to work it." Then the other voice, "Give me that . . ." The other guy must have hit a button on the camera then because there was no more audio on the tape after that. I was pretty sure they weren't aware anything had been recorded because there was no image, the lens cap must have been on the whole time.

"Too damn dumb," they'd said. I felt kind of lousy after hearing that line. It brought up a lot of memories. The teachers telling my mom about my needing to be put in special instruction at school. The kids laughing at me in the classroom. Here it was, almost twenty years later, and someone was still saying the same things about me. I guess nothing much had changed in the way people looked at me.

I didn't sleep too well that night. The next morning I found myself getting pretty upset over what I'd heard. I decided I needed to get this behind me, so I confronted Lerman over it. I walked up to him with the camera. I think Lerman just thought I had shot some footage of my house or something because he pointed to his watch and gave me a "Can't that wait?" look.

That's when I said, "Steve, I want you to listen to something on this video. At first I was just going to tape over it, but I decided it's something you've got to be aware of, and it's something I want us to deal with before we do any more business together." That got his attention. I hit the play button, with the volume up and you should have seen the look on his face when he heard the playback. Now Lerman didn't always see eye-to-eye with me, but his expression told me that he was as stunned as I was, and not because I was ready to stop working with him, but because he was honestly hurt by those words. He told me that it was inexcusable and that he would handle it. I wasn't sure what he did, but the next time I went back to the office, I didn't see that co-worker anymore. He was either gone or staying the hell out of my way.

ATTORNEY WITH A HEART

Nearly at the end of my rope and unsure of what to do next, I randomly received a call from the most unlikely source, offering to help me out. Evidently Fred Sayre, the medical specialist attorney that Grimes had brought on board, had had a big falling out with Grimes over his fees and the total amount he felt he deserved. Fred called me to say that Stanley Steinberg, an attorney from Orange County, was just the guy to reel in any funds due me.

After the disasters I'd been through with other attorneys, I wanted to make sure this Steinberg guy was as good as Fred claimed, so I went down to Steinberg's offices and had a face-to-face with him. Within ten minutes, I knew this was the right guy, though I'd felt that before and been proven badly wrong. He calmly told me his take on the challenges we faced and the proper way to recoup the amounts due me. He had already charted out a strategy to do this in a way that was constructive and not confrontational, although he made it clear this was going to take a very dedicated effort.

Then he began to tell me that he had followed every phase of my life from the night he saw the Holliday video to present day. I got chills, because this grown man began to weep openly in front of me. Far as I could tell, it wasn't an act. He wasn't bawling, but I watched as his eyes filled up and tears began to roll down his cheeks. He told me that he understood I was no saint, but I had opened an entire nation's eyes to the undeniable existence of police brutality and racial prejudice in law enforcement, and that was an incredible accomplishment for any one man. I should be proud of that, he said.

Well, I was proud that I had finally found this needle-in-a-haystack proper lawyer for the job. Steinberg got right on it, and what followed was one lawyer, Steinberg, taking a deposition from another attorney, Grimes. It felt right paying Stanley Steinberg $25,000 to settle the matter, if only that had been the case. But after another round of chasing our tails, I was no closer to collecting the balance of my monies than I had been before his tears started flowing.

Steinberg convinced me that the only way to get my money was to sue Steve Lerman for malpractice. In the suit that was filed in California's superior court, we claimed that Lerman had failed to comply with repeated requests to fully account for the $3.8 million in damages as a result of the beating. Steinberg also said that Lerman had engaged in a "series of intentional misrepresentations, deceits and concealments" with the intent of depriving me of my legal rights to my money.

I testified, "I feel like they took advantage of my lack of understanding of the law and resorted to their superior educational background to deceive, mislead and rob me out of monies that rightfully belong to me." That pretty much sums up my whole experience.

Around this time I remember getting a phone call from Al Sharpton.

"Everything all right?" he asked. I hadn't heard that jolly voice of his in a long time. "Everything good, Rodney?"

I didn't launch into everything, though part of me wanted to—wanted to tell him all about the lawyers and the money and the headaches and my wife and everything. Just to have somebody hear me out. But it was a quick call. And he had his own agenda anyway. He told me about an event coming up in New York, and we ended up in the same room at a black leaders' dinner in the city. But Sharpton never made an attempt to speak with me. He was surrounded all evening, though mostly by his entourage and suck-ups. I just felt silly sitting there because he was the reason I had agreed to fly out to New York, on my own dime, for the event. Maybe Mr. Sharpton wanted me to come up to the table and bear-hug him, but I wasn't about to do that.

In the end, I was out of luck because I was out of time. I had waited too damn long to file the malpractice suit against Steve Lerman, the first of the twenty-seven lawyers who had represented me since 1991. That was the ruling by the L.A. Superior Court Judge Ann Kough. Judge Kough ruled that Steinberg's claims against Lerman were barred by the one-year statute of limitations. Lerman had ceased representing me for over a year from the period I rehired him to go after my money. I had told Sayre, when he reached out to me after the Norman Grimes mess, that Lerman was no longer representing me in any capacity. I just could no longer trust him.

To this day, the words that haunt me the most were from the judge who looked at me and actually said out loud: "Why did you wait so long?" I needed to act right away. I should have. The moment that Maxine Waters told me that the city was sending the checks directly to Lerman or Grimes, I should have gotten on it immediately. I didn't and I regret that every day.

But my main problem was that I listened to people who I'm sure had good intentions. But everyone had an opinion, and no one knew how to handle the big picture. Every time I was referred to someone who could straighten it out, it just became more crooked, until I was back to square one, going in circles. When it was all over, after those twenty-seven attorneys made a run at my money, I ended up with less than half of my award, $1.7 million.

MARITAL PROBLEMS

The years of court battles and lawyers and stress took its toll on me mentally, and took its toll on my family and my marriage too. It seemed my wife, Crystal, would never stop talking about the money, why I was getting screwed, and why I needed to "step up" and get at least a couple million more. It led to a sad confrontation with my wife, an episode that was thoroughly humiliating, and a sign of how bad things had gotten.

By 1995, even though the legal wrangling had ended, my marriage had eroded to the point that she and I both wanted out. Or at least that's what I sensed, though neither of us had said as much out loud. We argued too much, and the most routine conversation could suddenly turn loud and ugly. And it was almost always about money. Our marriage was falling apart. And I was so upset and mentally frayed that I did the one thing that assured it would end: I began to see another woman who was from out of town, up in the Oakland area. She was beautiful and sweet and so easy to hang out with compared to my spouse.

But in a last-ditch effort to save my marriage I proposed we move away from all the chaos and settle in a better community, where Crystal and I could rebuild what had once been a loving relationship. She seemed interested, but I think it had more to do with moving into a bigger, nicer house than being with me.

Crystal had given birth to our beautiful baby girl, Uniqua, a perfect child that I absolutely worshipped. She was a source of strength and love for me during the most trying times, and I had only to look into those beautiful mahogany eyes to gather my nerves for another day. I used to tickle her permanently wet chin and she would erupt into giggles that were incredibly cute. It just lifted my heart right up.

After I said we should move to a better home, Crystal found a four-bedroom house about thirty miles north and we decided to drive up and check it out. Now I barely touched on this episode in the previous chapter, when I was charged with assault with a deadly weapon. I want to go into it more thoroughly, because I've never spelled out the whole story and the way it really happened.

On the way back we weren't really paying attention and got lost. Soon we began to disagree about the best way to turn around and get back on the highway, and it quickly became a screaming match. The arguing got so out of hand that I finally pulled over to the shoulder because I could not trust myself to drive safely any longer.

The yelling only got worse, which wasn't surprising because this was always the pattern. To be fair, Crystal had been through hell with me, and I believe she was storing up a lot of unresolved issues, so whenever we tangled over anything, it always just exploded into a lot of nonstop shouting.

It got so bad I told Crystal to get out of the car. I wasn't going to risk getting back on the road with her screaming at the top of her lungs into my ear. I told her we both needed to chill out before we got back on the road. She gladly got out of the car to smoke a cigarette. Then something came over me and I got so upset I just pulled out because I was positive I would get in an accident if Crystal and I continued on that day in the same car.

At the last second she must have realized she had left her purse on the passenger seat and reached in to the open window to snag it. I didn't see her reaching in because I was looking left at the street traffic to ease in. Well, when I pulled out, she stumbled and fell. I drove off. I was an idiot acting impulsively out of fear.

Just like so much else in my life, it all got blown out of proportion. When the police and papers heard "Rodney King" everything got twisted and amplified. I got so sick of it, but it was entirely my fault. I created the monster and I must live with it.

After the police spoke to several eye witnesses, I was charged with spousal battery, assault with a deadly weapon (the car), hit and run, and reckless driving. My attorney, David Lynn, called my arrest "the catch of the day" for the local police, and by the time trial proceedings began at the Alhambra Municipal court in July of 1996, the papers and TV reports were camped out, covering this day and night, and calling it a clear case of spousal abuse. Rodney King back in the news.

It repeated a familiar pattern where no police force or municipal court could resist using my name to get bigger headlines and greater coverage. If I did something stupid—no matter how small or big—they always wanted to make it as big a deal as possible. Lynn told the press that if I wasn't Rodney King, there would be absolutely no case. And Crystal, who had already forgiven me for what happened, and understood I wasn't trying to hurt her, said that it was precisely because of who I was that she had not wanted to press charges. She said she was afraid that if the incident was brought to trial, it could result in my facing twenty-five years to life under the three strikes law. I knew I had one strike, but I don't know how they came up with a second strike to make this one the potential third.

The Alhambra police huddled with Crystal because they suddenly had a biblical amount of patience to go over all the options for Crystal. They explained to her that the three-strikes law would not be a factor with this kind of charge. No ma'am, not at all. And so they talked Crystal into pressing charges.

When she took the stand to testify against me in court she told the lawyer that she filed for legal separation on July 15, 1995, the day after the incident. She said that she was waiting for divorce proceedings to begin in a few weeks and had hired a high-profile attorney, Gloria Allred, to represent her.

To her credit, she testified that she was not sure she was deliberately thrown off the car. And no matter how that lawyer tried to twist her words and make me look like an uncaring, destructive monster, Crystal would not say that I had set out to hurt her. Crystal was a woman scorned, and she was in a position where she could have punished me for my lust and stupid-ity, but I give her credit, she did not.

I HAD A DREAM

My goals were very simple, I wanted to gather up all the award money that I was legally entitled to and invest it in a way that I could proudly tell my mother and the rest of my family that we would never have to worry about money again. Since I still didn't have a job or any medical insurance, I really needed the money. I knew the money due me wasn't nearly enough for us to live in luxury, but it was enough—if we invested wisely and didn't touch the principle—to take care of food, shelter, educa-tion, and maybe even the medical necessities for my immedi-ate family. We just had to be smart, drive Camrys instead of Continentals, and hold down jobs to take care of extras for the kids, like nicer clothes or vacations.

My daughters, nieces, and nephews were all going to get a good education and learn how to compete and succeed in this cold, hard world. That's where I definitely tripped up in my youth, and I wasn't going to let that happen to my loved ones.

And if one of my investments brought in a bonus amount, then I wanted to go after a secret dream I had kept locked up my entire life. I wanted to find and support some kids who were musically gifted and create my own hip-hop band. And maybe, if that went well, and the band created some heat, my own hip-hop label. I love love love music. It lifted my spirits in the toughest times and, besides, I always wanted to do something like being a music producer to make my family proud of me.

That was my dream, and I held it very dear. And despite everything, all the years and battles and betrayals, I still believed something good might come out of all the pain.

Chapter 7

A NEW MAN

REBUILDING RODNEY

The verdict and the resulting riots tore everyone down and made us all rebuild again, not just the city and the police department, but me too. The whole ordeal resulted in a strong desire, on my part, to forge a new, more positive approach to who I was and what I was trying to be. Up to the beating and including the civil suits that followed, I had merely reacted to everything swirling around me and had not given myself a chance to sit down and really take stock of all that had happened in the last year. After all I had been through I realized I needed to stop feeling sorry for myself, and I needed to educate myself and go forward with a more positive attitude.

As the months rolled on, one of the things my mother noticed was that I was trying to be calmer and more realistic with what I could accomplish and who I could be. Rather than just being proof of the existence of police brutality and racism that existed among law enforcement officers in L.A., I could be a positive voice in the pursuit of racial harmony among the people of L.A. We had to come to terms with the fact that we were all human with flaws; we made mistakes. This could be a time of healing, we had to stop stoking our fears with prejudice and hate.

Time to lose the hate and bring on the love. Some of this new, healthier perspective came about when my wife, Crystal, and her family convinced me to change attorneys. That's when I let go of Steve Lerman and hired the attorney they recommended, Milton Grimes. Grimes was a more established lawyer and seemed to realize right away that I needed some positive grooming if we were going to work together successfully. He told me that having a strong sense of self was crucial whether I was in a civil suit or a three-piece suit. I could tell right away that this attorney had a better grip on the big picture, and that got me more determined to cooperate with him.

RESHAPING RODNEY

Although I've already touched on my tutoring briefly, I want to go into how it helped me to shift the way I began to look at myself. Grimes sat me down and told me it was all right to be angry as long as I channeled that displeasure into something productive. He seemed to see me as the perfect work in progress and immediately set up a tutor, Judy Sampson, whose job was to give me a sense of history about the black man. She began to teach me more about major black leaders such as Medgar Evers, Martin Luther King Jr., and Malcolm X. These men had sacrificed much in the advancement of our people. I seemed to gather strength as I learned more about them and the details of their amazing accomplishments. I was also taught how to conduct myself with the media, how to look people right in the eye, talk slowly, and nod. I was told not be afraid to ask someone to repeat a question if I didn't understand it completely or to insist they be clearer about something they said. After a while, I began to see how I might be a positive symbol too, but only if I could turn my life around.

Grimes set up a "war room" where he worked on strategies for the two remaining trials, and his plan to reshape my image going forward. African art lined the walls in this room and created an atmosphere that kept me mindful of where I came from and who I could become. There were new responsibilities that came with being a positive role model. Neither one of us would ever forget the beating or what the cops said to me that night, but this was all about turning the page. Grimes was careful when I first went before the cameras. Interviews were primarily before black journalists. I gave interviews on a black radio call-in show and we turned down a lot of interviews from reporters who had printed unfounded, damaging stories. This all raised my "black consciousness," which was one of Grimes's top priorities. Milton gathered together a group of black professionals to form a group called the Justice for King Committee. We held our meetings mostly at night and put together more long-range detailed plans that showed me how I could be a symbol for positive change and justice. Staying clean and surrounding myself with good people that I could trust was going to be key.

My attorney stayed in touch with the media and occasionally shared his optimism with my new attitude and improved image. At one point he told *Newsweek*, "Rodney King may not be a Medgar Evers or a Martin Luther King or a Malcolm X, but symbolically in young African-American minds he couldn't be more important. . . . You can't talk to a young African-American male who doesn't know of Rodney King. And their first comment is, 'I'm not taking a Rodney King ass-whippin'.'"

Part of this new image involved sacrifice. There were temptations out there that weren't lost on me. Grimes and I wanted to limit my appearances pretty much exclusively to black media. This wasn't going to be about the money, it was the message that counted. Meanwhile, Koon and Briseno were cleaning up. I was told that Phil Donahue paid them $25,000 each to appear on what must have been a very one-sided vanilla appearance on *Donahue*.

There wasn't a talk show or a news program that hadn't devoted a special, sometimes several of them, to what became known, around the world, as the Rodney King Incident. Even talk superstars like Oprah staged their own shows "live from Los Angeles" after the verdicts. But Oprah was cool—she opted for more of a town-hall type setting. She wanted to hear what the people had to say about that night, not me, not the cops, not the lawyers or politicians. That's why she is so beloved—she is real. She is what I was trying to become, true to my people, a positive role model.

But I was just an undereducated mess and needed all kinds of coaching to carry me through the federal trial and civil trials that pretty much consumed almost two years of my life from 1993 through the spring of 1994. Sometimes my head would feel like it was going to split open. I was still getting pretty severe headaches and was always stiff jointed. I couldn't sit still for more than five, ten minutes without having to start shifting around and eventually stand up out of my seat.

But I was still plenty young enough to fight the lasting effects of the beating. I started to exercise more regularly and to lose weight. I was determined to get into better shape, and it felt great. And the more I learned about black history, the more my attitude improved. Without being entirely conscious of it, I started to focus more on the future while letting go of the past.

Grimes believed psychiatric counseling would be beneficial and, after having my doubts, it did seem to help me with my outlook. I also began attending an alcohol rehab program to get my head clear and speed up getting into better shape. I should have begun with this step, because there was such a noticeable improvement in everything once I stopped drinking. I immediately felt so much better that I began initiating my own self-improvement. I got to work on the one area I thought would be toughest, fixing my marriage. My relationship with Crystal had been suffering from the trials and nonstop media glare. Crystal could be so sweet and so supporting, but I hadn't really given her a chance. I needed to step up and show her that I loved her and that she was a big reason for my counseling, physical fitness, and quitting drinking.

ROAD TO RAP

Finally, I turned my attention to one of my first loves, music. I began writing some black-pride lyrical poetry because one of my dreams had always been to start a rap label. This seemed to spark potential creative projects in other areas, and I was approached about a book and a movie deal. Nothing came of either, but it was cool just to think about the potential possibilities.

My tutor and I talked about another possibility: buying a farm. It was something I mentioned during our first few lessons together and she said that maybe my desire wasn't so much about me wanting to go out and plant vegetables or milk cows. She figured, probably rightly so, that it was more about my wanting to get away from it all. She was right, because as I stated in the previous chapter, Crystal and I began looking at homes that were a good ways from where we were living at the time. Unfortunately our trip to check out a large house ended in a damn catastrophe.

Things had been getting better for a good stretch, so I was just devastated when this happened between me and Crystal. Grimes started to lay a good foundation for me, but I was only able to build on it for a while, and then I stumbled.

But I didn't fall, because low or high, high or straight, I have always loved rap music. Rapping made me feel alive—it brought out the humor, the wisdom, and the passion in me. I remember the night I was beaten, we were doing some rapping earlier. Me and Pooh, one of the two guys in the car with me that evening, were going to form a rap group duo. We were at a recording studio and then later we wrote down some rap lyrics at a friend's house. In fact, I believe we were cruising to the chill beats of De La Soul when the car chase began.

I never did talk much about any of this after the arrest, even though the media constantly asked me for details: "Why didn't you stop? What were you thinking? Why didn't you hear the siren? Were you playing music? Was that it? So was the music too loud for you to hear the police? What music were you playing? Even if the music was too loud, you still could see the lights from the cop car, couldn't you?" And then back to "So why didn't you stop?" It was one big loop that they kept running over and over.

After a while it felt like it didn't matter what I said, they were going to keep asking the question regardless of the answer. Why didn't I stop? I told you, I didn't want to go to jail for breaking my parole. Or maybe I don't have a reason. Have you ever done anything stupid in your life and didn't know why? That was me that night. I knew it wasn't right to keep driving but I did it anyway.

ROMANCE WITH RAP

After I got the $1.7 million in award money, I set out to do something about this dream to create a rap studio. All my high-minded intentions to do something for my family took a backseat. I reshuffled my priorities because the one thing I thought that would take a lot of time, finding a talented rap group, was suddenly right there in front of me. I didn't really know what to do next, but I knew what not to do. I turned down all future interviews and appearances. I told *USA Today*, "I just want to bring it all to a closure . . . I can see that night . . . when I start talking about it. . . . I kind of start looking off in a daze. You know?" It was time to move on from that night. The whole world knew my name, so getting publicity for the label was probably not going to be a problem. I just had to concentrate on the *music*. I wanted this to happen so badly. And besides, if we had a hit I could really take care of my family while still making great music.

After the beating, and everything else, finding material for the rap group was not going to be a problem. I was even planning a new version of N.W.A.'s "F*** Tha Police" with rapper Eazy-E. But then suddenly we had to put the whole rap thing on hold. We were still dealing with some legal issues, and my attorneys told me to dial it down, way down. I guess they were afraid a potential jury member might hear the rap lyrics and be offended. Also, the untimely death of my partner, Pooh, and lingering problems with my injuries kind of killed the momentum.

By 1998, I had the desire back, had scouted some new talent, and was ready to get back on track with what had to be done. Out of a small home office, with my own money, I started my rap label. I called it Straight Alta-Pazz Recording after the neighborhoods I grew up in, Altadena and Pasadena, California. We had some initial success too. The hip-hop group Stranded released a song called "Do It How U Wanna," which was played on a bunch of rap radio stations. But don't let anyone tell you that the recording industry got rid of the illegal, unethical practice of paying to have your music played on the radio, what they called payola. Because let me tell you, it is still alive and well. And the costs were ridiculous just to have one song played a couple of times on a major station. Maybe they don't call it payola any more, but it's still going on and someone is making a bundle.

I wasn't bitter, however, because I was in it to win it. I never worked harder in my life, and I was never happier. I tried to follow the rap artists who had a track record I admired. I liked Sean "Puffy" Combs. I liked the way he operated, finding great rappers and bringing them to his label. That's how it went down with Stranded. I liked them, I gave them a home, and we created a hot disc that will be around forever. I believe every man's got to leave a piece of himself on this planet before he dies, and with me one of the things I'm proudest of is Stranded's debut album, titled *4/29/92*, which of course is dedicated to the start date of the riots. Having that song, "Do It How U Wanna," play on the radio was one of my proudest moments and one of the most important things I have ever accomplished.

My rap company had eight people in it, but no one had that much experience in the record industry. I didn't mind—I wanted people I knew I could trust. The music business takes a lot of cunning, money, and muscle. I had some connections in the industry. In fact my second wife, Dede, was cousins with Mac 10. We used to call him little Monty. I remember when he was just a sweet young kid and his grandmother used to drop him off with us.

The story I heard was that Mac 10 was brilliant the way he used his resourcefulness to move up the ladder in the rap business. He wrote a letter to the Muslim brothers who had access to Ice Cube. He spoke passionately to Cube and told him in the letter that he was close to the persecuted black man Rodney King, and that in fact his dear cousin Dede was Rodney's wife. Whether this actually was what got him in to meet Cube, I'll never know for sure. But Monty was smart and resourceful, and made the most of the opportunity. He became a protégé of Cube, who began to feature Mac 10 in his shows.

I love and respect Cube. He is the only rapper who had the balls to call out them officers by name in his lyrics: "Fuck Laurence Powell and Briseno, Wind and Koon, pretty soon / We'll fuck them like they fucked us and won't kiss 'em." The fact is, Cube has been saying "fuck the police" from the beginning. Ice Cube's third solo album, *The Predator*, was recorded during the height of racial tensions in L.A.

I believe some of his work was influenced by the Rodney King Incident, because when Cube actually dropped my name in one of his greatest raps, "We Had to Tear This Mothafucka Up," his timeless homage to the L.A. riots: "You had to get Rodney to stop me cos you know what? / We woulda teared this muthafucka up."

The only thing that made me sad was when I went to someone in the music industry and asked for a little help with getting one of my acts as a feature on a show. It sounded like it was going to happen, but at the last minute, they pulled my band, Stranded, from the showcase. I was told that I didn't have enough money to get my group the serious promotion they needed. They asked me how much I was willing to spend on Stranded, and when I said $200,000, they almost laughed at me and said I needed at least $500,000 just on ads and promotion for a band. I needed to understand that such discussions were just part of the entertainment business. The fact is that I never got the best advice about how to launch a band, and needed to figure a lot out for myself.

One of the biggest lessons I learned was that making it in the music business is a whole lot harder than it looks. It takes so much money just to make music move, just to get it out there! I had no idea. That's why I'm proud that I produced the Stranded album *4/29/92*. I didn't want to be known for just delivering the message "Can we all just get along?" That was just the start of my desire to keep getting out as many positive messages in as many different ways as possible.

Having my own studio and eventually going bust was an amazing ride. I have no regrets and learned a lot. I'm pretty sure I would do it all again, but definitely not the same way. I got to touch my dream, and that's more than I can say for a lot of people, who talk the talk but that's it. The fact that I chose to try and make it in one of the dirtiest, most unethical businesses on the planet was just the price of admission. I love music, and maybe one day, I'll be able to take another shot.

UP AND DOWN

After the Straight Alta-Pazz label collapsed, so did I. Maybe all the stress and disappointment got to me, or maybe it was being the poster child for civil rights that was getting to me, but I just lost control. In 1999, I got arrested again for spousal abuse. There was something tragic and sad about the fact that Mac 10 had thrown it in my face and now it was happening all over again. I got into more hot water in 2001 with three counts of being under the influence of PCP and one count of indecent exposure. Although I was not on PCP the night of the beating, the drug had eventually gotten its hooks into me. It is one of the most disorienting, destructive substances a person can put into their body and I was a complete mess. In my depression and despair it looked like I just wanted to tear everything back down again. I was ordered to undergo a year of drug treatment.

I'd get out of treatment, think I was getting some traction, and then I'd get in another wreck, literally. That was in 2003 when I was arrested for speeding and running a red light under the influence of alcohol. My car slammed into a building, and the impact broke my pelvis.

My hip stayed pretty screwed up following the car crash. After getting out of the hospital and then serving time in jail, I still walked with a limp. By this point, I had moved to Rialto, a suburb east of L.A., first in a large house but then a smaller, more manageable one. I was really trying to keep it together and mind my own business, just stay out of trouble. I lived with my brother and daughter, and was close with my mom and my manager, David Guzman, who was still trying to do something with the rap music I had produced. But by then the award money was practically gone, and what money I had left was coming from a small mutual fund.

As much as I tried to keep a low profile, I kept finding myself on the wrong side of the law. And though I had tried repeatedly to get off the stuff, I could not completely stop with the angel dust. I simply behaved irrationally on the stuff, and had no ability to walk away from it. Drugs have always been my downfall, and I told the press: "PCP really got me into a wreck."

Like I stated, I wasn't hopped up on PCP the night I got pulled over and beaten. The blood tests that came back proved I was telling the truth, 0 percent in my body. I wrote a rap song about the whole horrible incident and called it "Beat Down." Guzman and I went around to try to find some investors to get it off the ground.

BOOK ABOUT MY LIFE

I was also working on the idea of a book about my life, but just when I got to the point that I could begin writing it, something always happened to screw it all up. At least I figured I'd have lots of material for when that day to get it all down finally came. And I've always wanted to tell my story my way, emphasizing what I know is important to me, and how I really felt during the entire ordeal. And by the end of 2011 I was so thrilled to finally be getting it all down.

In addition to the book proposals, I received one of the strangest pitches I'd ever heard in my life, and I'd heard some strange ones (including being asked to pose for *Playboy Magazine*). This one definitely topped them all: a boxing match against Officer Powell, one of the police who beat me on that night more than ten years ago—I was told that Powell agreed to fight me.

To my surprise, and a lot of other people's, I said I'd do it. I trained for it, and I applied myself to the point that I was ready. Powell looked fit enough at the trial, but I was going to have my day in the ring with this son of a bitch. It was payback time, but it really wasn't. The event never took place. I was told that Powell backed out.

SHOT WHILE BIKING

The Powell fight was probably the strangest thing that never happened to me. The strangest thing that ever actually happened to me was in late November of 2007. I was riding my bike and, out of nowhere, was shot by a shotgun. I swear my brother Gailen has premonitions that always prove true. He saw me on the bike and said, "I wouldn't go there, Glen. Not a good spot." It was late at night, around eleven P.M. I believe, and I was near the border of the San Bernardino and Rialto neighborhoods. The pellets came out of nowhere and slammed into my face, arm, and back. It hurt like hell, and only the sheer terror of what might happen to me if I fell off my bike kept me up and racing back home as fast as I could. We called the cops, and then I went to the hospital. The cops thought I had been drinking and were not able to put together any helpful leads from what I told them. Luckily shotgun pellets do not penetrate and damage the way a bullet might have, and I was able to heal up after the blast.

The fact is that I had been drinking that day and every day until things started to get out of hand again. My commitment to AA had completely collapsed, and nothing else seemed to be working. After recovering from the shotgun injuries, I was approached by a guy who coincidently was from AA, but this was about another program. I thought it was a dumb idea at first, but the more I worked it over in my head, the more I felt I had nothing to lose.

So in May 2008, I checked into a recovery center. This time, however, there were television cameras following me wherever I went. I was now part of the cast on the second season of a VH1 TV show called *Celebrity Rehab with Dr. Drew*. The group was pretty varied with people like Gary Busey, Jeff Conaway, Rod Stewart's son Sean Stewart, Tawny Kitaen, and Amber Smith. The following year, in 2009, I also appeared on the premier season of their spin-off show, titled *Sober House*. It was quite an experience, with many disappointing and many rewarding days. I've devoted a whole chapter to it and have kept up a good friendship with Dr. Drew since the show first aired.

In fact, by March of 2009, I was going on nine months of sobriety. I was so proud of that fact. It had not been easy. The local news station in Los Angeles, KCAL News, interviewed me. I still didn't like doing these types of shows, because they usually tell you their objective is to focus on a certain subject that they know I'll agree on, but then, when the interview begins, their true intentions are revealed, and it's usually controversial crap that's never pleasant for me. But I agreed to sit down with their reporter. I told her about how I felt my life was finally at a solid resting point. She asked me about my father dying when he was forty-two. I told her I didn't want that to be my fate. I was a grandpa now! I had a lot to look forward to. That interview was one of the better experiences I've had, because I got to say what we had agreed to discuss.

FIGHT NIGHT

With my sobriety came more energy and a new willingness to get in the best shape ever. The Laurence Powell match had grabbed my interest, even though it never came together. So I started to look into other celebrity boxing match opportunities. I found them fun, good exercise, and a great outlet for burning off whatever might be bugging me at the time. When I was forty-three years old, I participated in a boxing match with a guy nearly twelve years younger than me. He was named Simon Aouad, but for the fight he went by "The Renegade." This guy was a real special case. Like Powell, he was a former police officer, and I heard he had been kicked out of the force a few years ago for following a "shoot first, ask questions later" policy when someone broke in to his property.

The fight was at the Ramada Philadelphia Airport in Essington, Pennsylvania, on September 11, 2009. It was broadcast on pay-per-view. We fought in front of a live audience that paid $25 per ticket. To hype the event, both Aouad and I did some publicity. I took the entire thing as an opportunity to get in the ring, make some money, and have a good, fair fight. Again, I have always thought of these things as fun. But I think Aouad took it much more seriously. For example, we did an interview on Philly's Fox local news, and they had us both on. Aouad wore his sunglasses the entire time and had a chain around his neck. He never broke character as "The Renegade," whoever that was, and said I should get ready for a "beating."

Then, at a press conference for the fight, he was seated to my right. We were separated by one person. While I was talking, he leaped up from the table and tried to put his hands on me. The handlers calmed him down.

I knew some people would see me and a cop going at it all over again as anything from pathetic to hilarious. But I kept telling anyone who would listen that I would box with anyone who was worthy to fight me. While the event is fun for me, I am very competitive in sports, whether on a diamond or ringside. And for this fight, I had never felt better, either physically or mentally.

And I proved it that night. All of The Renegade's theatrics didn't do him much good when it came to stepping in the ring. I was relentless, using the ring to cut off his dancing around. And I beat him, fair and square.

At these celebrity boxing matches, they have all kinds of characters, as you can imagine. I even did an interview for a show called *The Herbie Herb Show* before a match in Springfield, Massachusetts. On November 6, I was set to face David Fresko, a six-foot, seven-inch former basketball player.

I remember talking to an ESPN writer in the hallway before the fight. She asked me about the defining moment of my athletic career. I told her about one of the first times I tried playing baseball, mainly at the outfield and third base positions. "We came in first place. I still remember it felt so good to be on a team and win. It was in Pony League baseball with the Sierra Madre Cardinals. I think it was 1976."

Thinking back, that was when the fitness bug really bit me. Even now nearly thirty years after the baseball start, I still loved breaking a sweat. And even more, I loved to win. There is nothing like victory in sports. That night I won by technical knockout in the second round, defeating the former basketball player.

This was a nice high point in my life. I was in good shape and more importantly, I had seventeen months of sobriety under my belt. I'm sure some people thought I couldn't box, and honestly, I'm probably not that good. But it just felt so darn good to be in the ring. So many things that had happened over the years were just a blur, so I really tried to drink in every moment now. That same month I also fought Bob Meloni and Jose Canseco.

In 2009, I was also invited back to *Celebrity Rehab*, this time as an alumnus of the program, a sober alumnus. I joined other alumni to appear as panel speakers to talk to a new group of addicts at the Pasadena Recovery Center.

BACK IN LOVE

In 2010, I reunited with a former girlfriend. Her name is Cynthia Kelley. We rediscovered a bond that most people did not understand. Cynthia was actually a juror during the civil trial that resulted in a decision to award me the $3.8 million. In the court papers, she was known as Juror #5.

We got back together, and around the end of the summer, I proposed. I was so excited when she said yes. She was such a blessing to me. I don't know what I would have done without her, and I can't wait to make her my wife!

We had to keep it secret when we first got together right after the trial ended. At the time we were both married to other people. Our first date wasn't exactly the most romantic—it was the day after the trial. Me and my lawyer went to see Cynthia at a pizza place in Newport Beach.

We ended up separating during my time on VH1's *Celebrity Rehab*, but I never forgot her. So, in 2010, I picked up the phone and called her and just hoped she was still single, and she was! It had been many years since we spoke, but as soon as we reconnected, it was like a day had never passed. There's a bit of a romantic in me, and I thanked the Lord that I could pick up my very special love with Cynthia again.

ANOTHER SETBACK

In March 2011, I suffered a setback when I was stopped by L.A. police for driving erratically and issued a citation for driving with an expired license. It was very unfortunate timing because it all happened right around the twentieth anniversary of the beating.

For anniversary observance, I agreed to participate in a CNN special. I went back to the scene where it had all begun two decades before, and conducted part of the interview from there. Maybe one day the city will recognize that spot, officially, as a place to pray for people of all colors to get along better.

I opened up a bit for the CNN interview. I finally told the truth about the fact that I was going every bit of 100 mph, the top speed that Hyundai claimed that vehicle could reach. I didn't want to stop because I was on parole. Earlier that day I had gotten word that my old construction company wanted me to come back to work that next Monday, and I desperately wanted to start work again. I had been drinking that night, and I knew I would be arrested.

As I took the exit for the CNN documentary people, my heart raced, just as it had that night. I told them I had known I would get a beating for running from the LAPD at that point. I just felt it. I retraced what I had done for the CNN cameras, from me getting out of the car and on the ground to when I was first nailed in the head. I showed them how I had to blow blood out of my sinuses and spit it out of my mouth so I could breathe. I remember seeing my reflection in a window. I just started crying and said to myself, "I'll never look normal again."

When I found out that the beating had been caught on tape, I thought maybe I had a chance. During the trial, I wasn't concerned. I just knew justice would be served. There was the tape, you just had to look at it! But incredibly that wasn't enough, and all four cops walked.

I confided to the CNN crew that I still suffered from nightmares. At forty-five years old, I have to keep exercising to keep my muscles from stiffening. The easiest question he asked me was what I would have done differently that night. I just smiled and said I would have stayed home. Yes, I would have definitely stayed home that night.

Chapter 8

CLEAN AND SOBER

I'M AN ALCOHOLIC

They make you say that every time you go to an AA meeting, and God knows I've been to my share. But you can introduce yourself as an alcoholic without believing it's the truth. It was a courageous day when I finally accepted that I was an alcoholic, and had been one for a long time. It was equally brave for me to realize that AA wasn't working for me.

Nothing was working for me, but I'd tone it down until I felt I was doing fine. Then I'd believe I could handle a few drinks and this would lead to a cycle of terrible days, sometimes weeks, when I drank so much I lost my grip on reality. If there was any hope for my dealing with the demon alcohol it was when things got so bad, there was no way they could get worse. They call it rock bottom. Then my choices were brutally simple, either get clean or get dead.

Almost two decades after my battered image was splashed all over every TV set in the nation, my face was appearing again on a nationally televised show. The popular VH1 show about addiction, *Celebrity Rehab,* reached out to me as a potential cast member. I guess they do it through the celebrity's family, friends, agents, and managers. In my case, I was talking to the show's people way before I met Dr. Drew. In fact, I was first approached about being on the second season of *Celebrity Rehab* by someone who had been a sponsor for AA. I told him I wasn't really all that interested. It just didn't strike me as the best way, or even a good way, to get cleaned up.

It bugged me that someone from AA, an organization based on the importance of anonymity, was talking to me about cleaning up on cable TV. Let's face it, if you need to be in front of millions of viewers with a camera crew in your face every minute of the day, you've got your priorities for getting sober pretty screwed up. But the money wasn't bad and since I was taking a break from AA to look for a more effective program, why not?

So I became a cast member on season two of *Celebrity Rehab* with Dr. Drew Pinsky, who's one of the executive producers of the show. The other addicts in rehab with me were Gary Busey, Amber Smith, Tawny Kitaen, Steven Adler, Sean Stewart, Nikki McKibbin, and Jeff Conaway. Gary was a pretty famous actor who was a recovering cocaine addict. Amber was a model/actress who was addicted to opiates. Tawny was an actress who was addicted to painkillers, cocaine, and sleeping pills. Steven was the founding drummer for Guns N' Roses, and his addiction was primarily to heroin. Sean was the son of Rod Stewart, and he was addicted to alcohol, coke, Vicodin, and heroin. Nikki was a singer who was a finalist on *American*

Idol, and she was addicted to alcohol and coke. Jeff was an actor immortalized by his great performance co-starring with John Travolta in *Grease.* He suffered from debilitating joint pain that led to his addiction to painkiller opiates for easing his condition.

I used to push Jeff around the *Celebrity Rehab* home in his wheelchair. It became the only way he could get around the rehab center. He died in May 2011 of pneumonia and sepsis. I was very sad when I heard the news. I felt bad that in the end, he lost his battle and the drugs took him down.

God Bless you Jeff, RIP.

GETTING CLEAN

On the first day of rehab, I showed up at the Pasadena Recovery Center late in the morning. I rolled up in a light blue Hud & Sons Towing truck. I was working part time for Hud & Sons with friends I've known since I was a kid. In the first episode of *Celebrity Rehab,* I introduced myself and said I'm just a down-to-earth guy, but I was stuck in time. For some reason, I became very jittery and nervous in front of the camera. I was sweating and had to continuously wipe my forehead. I had a bottle of beer handy, and I tilted my head back and chugged a good amount. That settled me down a bit, and I remember saying that life was good as long as I could wake up to a beer.

Brian and Corey, my friends over at Hud & Sons, were interviewed, and Corey stepped up that day and said, "When he's sober, he's nice and calm. No problems. Everybody loves him.

And when he gets a little alcohol in him, he gets a little wild." It was like I was two different people, Corey said. The camera followed me on the job and filmed me when I was drunk, so there are shots of me looking tipsy on a rig, saying I wanted a beer, and almost getting crushed by a car as I'm laying on the ground because I won't move over. I also threw up out the passenger window at one point when I was riding in the truck.

I was so desperately tired of all that. I was forty-three, and it was high time for me to have the courage to change, to stop my abuse and addiction to alcohol by getting it the hell out of my life. I honestly wanted to get clean, AA wasn't working, and I decided, on the drive over, to really give *Celebrity Rehab* my best shot. While still in the car, I had a thought that made me kind of fearful for the first time: I began to believe I was running out of time and that this had to work. It was the first time that I realized—no, not realized—accepted, that the booze had total control over me and had been toying with me for over a decade, making me think I could get off it at any time.

When I arrived at *Celebrity Rehab,* I regretted my promise to stick it out almost immediately. I hadn't been in the house two minutes when Gary Busey basically threatened me. He told me not to fuck with his women. He said I wasn't even supposed to look at them because they were his girls and they wanted nothing to do with a loser like me. I thought he was messing with me at first. He had that super intense expression on his face, like he was in the middle of taking a painful dump. I didn't know if he was playing me or not. His eyes were buggin', and I was like "the hell with this," so ready to walk out of there.

But I promised myself, right then and there, to give it at least a week. My first chat with Dr. Drew went pretty good. "So what the hell," I thought. "Worst-case scenario, learn what you can, cash the check, and move on." Dr. Drew and I talked about what I wanted to get out of the show and how I thought it would be best to carry on with my life after I was done with the show. We came up with the idea of revisiting the spot by the Children's Hospital where the LAPD had beaten me, and completely forgiving those officers for what they had done to me.

THE CONSTANT RIOT

That was the first time I told anyone about the riot churning inside me, and we talked about how letting go of the hate might go a long way to calming down the way I felt. I needed to quiet the unrest inside before I could work on the outside. Dr. Drew made a lot of sense, but he doesn't preach, and I guess that's what I like the most about him. He presents you with your situation and makes your options very clear, but he does not push for a certain outcome. I know I could have told him that I wasn't ready to forgive those cops and he would've understood.

Hate just gets inside you and messes you up. I loved my daddy, but I used to hate the way he drank all the time. I'd get so upset when he pushed around Momma and my little sister. Get that tight feeling in my chest, and sometimes, I swear, it felt like I was drowning. During the show when we had our group discussions, I kept flashing back to my daddy, Kingfish, who died so young. He just plain wore out from being a miserable alcoholic. I wondered if he ever had the fear of booze that was starting to creep up on me.

Dr. Drew asked me how much alcohol I drank in a day. I said a lot. I told him my dad died at forty-two, so I got him beat by a year. Dr. Drew told the camera later that he felt I knew I could end up dead because of drinking. He said one important step to make while I was in rehab was to process my feelings about the beating. He said he was surprised that I didn't discuss the beating during our first session until he brought it up.

I got that tight feeling just thinking about discussing the damn beating with him, with anyone. I don't think anyone understands how worked up I get when asked to talk about that night. Right now, just writing about it, I can feel my heart beating faster. People don't say, "Tell us about the night you were mugged . . ." "Tell us about your kid getting hurt . . ." "Tell us about your mother's funeral. . . ," but they have no problem asking me to relive the beating.

Well I told him exactly how I felt about that. I said that was years ago and it wasn't something I could talk about easily. Besides, I wasn't in such a good mood that day. It became obvious when Tawny Kitaen tried to introduce herself to me. She can be a very sweet person, and I didn't want to be rude, but I was not up for any chitchat. So I said hi quickly, then told her I really needed a drink of water and brushed by her to rush inside. She evidently turned to the camera and said this was going to be tough.

On the second day, we were still at the very start of the detox program. Dr. Drew said everyone cleans up differently—the rate we detox and how thoroughly we purge the poisons from our systems depend greatly on the particular substance we have been abusing and each individual's state of health, both physical and mental. Some people have a very tough time, particularly during the first week, and others have an easier go of it.

Nikki was one of those having a real hard time. She felt sick all the time, with no let up. Amber was super nervous in the early stage. Dr. Drew pointed out that opiate withdrawal can be one of the hardest: night sweats, deep muscle ache, and inability to focus. Looking around, judging everyone else's hardship and progress, it seemed my detox was going pretty well. If you looked at those episodes, I seemed unaffected. Don't let it fool you—I thought about how great it would be to sneak off with forty ounces of Old English every minute of every day. Just one good gulp and I'd be satisfied, until I wanted another one. But I felt I knew the drill well enough to just keep doing stuff to distract me.

The worst thing is to just sit and suffer. Time moves very slowly, and it makes the withdrawal period feel like an eternity. At one point I even realized that if I could do something to kick my ass a little, it would help take my mind off of it even more. That's why there's a shot of me working out on the elliptical machine during the detox period. I looked like all was well, but I was just trying to get my mind off of thinking about booze 24-7. And it worked too. I felt great when I got off the elliptical, but only for an hour or so. Then the evil thoughts started to creep back in.

Dr. Drew helped by providing us with a treatment routine that began every day with morning meditation. This was followed by a session called group process, which focused on emotional hang-ups and the work we'd need to clean that baggage up. The whole point of morning meditation was to remind us that recovery was our primary and only focus at this point in our lives. We couldn't be worrying about a mortgage payment, a sick relative, or the cost for new brake lining and hope to get through this.

The point of the process group, according to Dr. Drew, was also to "harness the power of many" and use it to confront and deal with addiction. Power in numbers—I got that and agreed that it's easier to take on a difficult foe when you've got people by your side willing to join in.

Poor Nikki looked really sick and could barely keep her eyes open in one of our early group sessions. I think that the worst part of withdrawal, the real demon factor, was when you thought you had gotten over the hump, because you actually felt almost normal when you woke up, or at least done with the rough stuff. And then *wham,* the cramps, sweats, and headaches came charging back in with all the shitty thoughts to accompany them. And just when you felt like the worst was over. That could be devastating.

I kept pretty quiet during this time. I'm no stranger to pain, and I knew that it was a lot like a sleeping dog. Leave it alone. The less noise I made, the less I bitched, the better.

Why throw light on it, wake it up, all raging and ready for another go-round? Dr. Drew looked around and told us withdrawal is like mourning. It's like the grief you feel when you lose someone, and that's what our bodies were experiencing. I never thought of it that way, and at first I wasn't sure it was very accurate. Mourning was about sadness, and that feeling was a distant third to the rage and fear I think most of us were experiencing.

Talk about rage—when we went to visit the woman at the meds counter, Jeff got mad and complained that he was in a lot of pain and wanted to leave and see his girlfriend, who was trying to get sober in another part of the rehab center. It was just addict babble, saying anything to get the hell out of there and pop a Percodan. I saw a cool side of Busey when he approached Jeff and talked him into pushing those thoughts out of his head and staying in rehab. Then I offered to help Jeff out by rolling him around, wherever he wanted to go in the house, in his wheelchair. Power in numbers, right?

Those were the coolest moments, namely when we took something Dr. Drew was trying to teach us and ran with it. He tipped off his satisfaction with us by smiling, but only very slightly. And if you weren't looking right at him at that very second, you would miss it. I caught it when I grabbed hold of Jeff's wheelchair, but that's because I was looking right at him, behaving like a student who wants the teacher to approve of what he's doing. It's a very insecure side of me, but any sign of approval can keep me going for days. Shine that apple—here, Teach.

At one point, Amber got really sick. I guess her detox was turning out to be the hardest one to go through. It got so bad, she literally collapsed in the hallway. She was twitching and sweating so badly that a medical attendant gave her a waste basket. He knew she couldn't move to the bathroom on her own. Amber tried to throw up to make herself feel better, but nothing came out, and she just laid on the floor. Dry heaves are the worst, and you can tear a stomach muscle retching away violently when there is just nothing to get out.

ROUGH GOING

After a couple or three days, it looked like Gary might be trouble. He seemed to be in an outright case of denial. He really believed, or at least wanted the cast to believe, he was there not as a patient, but because he was brought on the show to help the rest of us out with our addictions. I guess that's what he was told. But Gary definitely had a problem. He just didn't want to admit it to himself or anybody else. One day he told the camera crew that he didn't like being recorded. He fought against being filmed and did not want a microphone anywhere on him. At one point, he even pushed a cameraman.

But despite all these mini dramas going on around us, we decided, on the fourth day, to address the problems behind our addiction. Everyone began to open up and bare their soul, except Gary. He was just getting more and more ornery. Steven

Adler thought it was unfair that during one of our morning meditation sessions, Gary didn't even bother to show up. He was just sleeping in.

So me, Steven, and Sean decided to go to his room and wake him up. It didn't do any damn good. Gary made a show of getting up, then went right back to bed as soon as we left his room. To Steven's credit, he did not give up. He went after Gary during our group session and said he needed to wake up when everybody else did. They went back and forth at each other, these two blond boys, and after a while it just got ridiculous. I just smiled and laughed it off a little, because it was obvious Steven wasn't going to get anywhere. Gary was acting like an irrational, scared child. But I still wanted to like this guy because even when he was in his little fantasy mode, believing that he was there to help Dr. Drew get us off drugs, there was something touching about Gary. There's an innocence there that I think is genuine, and it makes for a beautiful human being until the drugs get in there and mess everything up.

That's why my mom taught me to always look for the good. It's too easy to find the evil, but since the Bible says that we are all made in His image, then we should look for the divine at all times. There was a lot of good in every one of those people on *Celebrity Rehab*. Dr. Drew believed that, and I did too. I think he sensed that we shared that view, and it made us a little tighter.

GETTING SERIOUS

Bob Forrest, a counselor who was in the group sessions with us and Dr. Drew, decided to go around the room and ask each of us what we thought our underlying problems were. He turned to me and asked me what I thought my main problem was. I said drinking and using, but mainly making the same dumb mistakes that caused me to get pulled back into that crazy world. That was what was tripping me up. Then I said I was constantly thinking about my kids. Dr. Drew jumped in and asked me what I thought my kids felt about me being an addict. I openly admitted my addiction was hurting my daughters, my mother, my whole family.

Bob said that being sober for my family wasn't enough. I needed to be sober for myself because that would help me stay sober. I needed to strip it down to the core. It sounds nice to say you're doing it for your kids, but if you want it to stick, it has to be about doing it for yourself. You must love yourself enough to beat your addiction, and then you can reach out and meaningfully love others.

Sean spoke up and said that his dad, Rod Stewart, wasn't around when he was growing up because he was always on tour, and his dad being gone still affects him as a grown man of twenty-seven. I could see the pain not having your dad with you can cause, and I got a bit teary eyed, because I knew what it was like to have problems with your father. Sean said he wasn't pissed at his dad, but he was hurt.

Dr. Drew said Sean's resentment was fueling his addiction. Sean needed to burn some of that off, and there's no better way than a good physical workout. That's when we all came up with the idea of Sean getting in the ring with me for some kickboxing. I had done a bunch of those celebrity boxing exhibitions in the last decade. Sean thought it was a good idea and really got into preparing for our little match. They even brought on Billy Blanks, the Tae Bo guy, to offer instruction. He worked with all of us at one time or another. However buff he looks on TV, he's even more cute in person!

Now this is kind of sad, but the morning before the fight, Sean's talking to his mom on the phone. He tells me his mom wants to talk to me. I get on the phone and the lady tells me to "go easy on my boy . . . don't hurt him." What the hell? I felt like calling it quits right then and there. It was that kind of stuff that put me off about the show. It might be preaching one thing, but it's really only ever after another—the show's ratings.

When Steven Adler asked his mom to come in for family weekend, they made a big deal of bringing Deanna Adler on the show to bury the hatchet with her son. I guess Steven hadn't been speaking with his mom for a long time. But the promos they telecast kept showing Steven throwing his hands up and storming out of the room in a complete rage. They knew that would get lots more eyeballs on their show. What threw me was the questions they asked the two of them seemed to invite hostility instead of healing, and that's where the show is definitely hypocritical.

The girls, Amber, Nikki, and Tawny, kind of kept their distance, probably because Busey had them all freaked out over me for no reason. They would nod and kind of smile at me, but I could tell they were just trying to be polite. Of the entire cast, Jeff Conaway and Steven Adler were the best. They were real decent to me.

Steven probably talked to me the most and was always real pleasant, a sweet guy. He was what my momma used to call sloppy clean. Shower three times a day, but his room looked like a typhoon hit it. There was a sad side to Steven that kind of broke my heart, but I really liked the way he looked right at me when he talked. That boy has been through some nasty shit, and I wish him well. He is into music, my favorite thing, and he is still playing in his own band, to his credit. He gives people exactly what they want, the greatest hits from that first GNR album, *Appetite for Destruction*.

Of the entire group, no one could make me laugh like Jeff. He had me bent over, cracking up one day. We had to take a shuttle bus out somewhere, and when I got on, I just went to the rear seats, mainly because I'm tall and that's the one place I can stretch out. Well, Jeff took exception to that. He was yelling at me to sit in the front of the bus. He was saying the American Civil Rights Movement been working for fifty years, since Rosa Parks, to get black people to the front of the bus, and there I was going to sit in the back again. "Rodney get on up here! That ain't right, now. You get on up here!" He had the whole bus laughing.

FACE THE MUSIC

Dr. Drew said trauma was one of the biggest factors in addiction and we had to address the beating aggressively. Dr. Drew paid me a huge compliment—he thanked me for being "such a rock" for everybody else in the rehab group. I knew he was building up my ego so we could have a meaningful discussion about the beating, but he was also sincere about what he said. I told him I was just being me, and that offering support for the others in the group was my way of shoring up my own confidence. The fact was that I sincerely appreciated what he said.

I still didn't want to talk about the beating, but Dr. Drew was pretty determined to draw it out of me. He said he couldn't believe that it wasn't still burning inside me. I told him that it was, but I didn't really care to go in there and stir it up much. He said this was my chance to tell him about it and that he would really like me to open up if I could. I felt the conflict within me, but that was when I asked myself, "What am I doing on this show if I'm not willing to listen to the doctor?" So what the hell, I started telling him about that night as honestly and completely as I could.

I told him about how young I was, how happy to have my old job back in construction. I told him how I was celebrating a little, partying with my buddies, and the happier I got, the more I drank. Until I was too drunk to know how drunk I was. I was supposed to start work on Monday, and this job was supposed to be a lot better than my last job, which was working at a paper company for $5.50 an hour.

Now that I was telling it all to Dr. Drew, having to say it all out loud, I could remember just how I felt that night. At that point in my life, I felt like I was the strongest I'd ever been. I was really thrilled at the thought of getting a paycheck again, and when I'm feeling great, I'm buying. I told my buddies to get in the car, that I felt like going for a drive, so they did. I remember wanting to go out to a spot where my dad used to take me fishing. I didn't know it then, but those would be the last few moments of my normal life. A few too many drinks, a few bad decisions, and nothing would ever be the same.

While I was telling Dr. Drew, I could almost remember the feeling of that night, the air coming through the windows. I could almost hear the music playing loud on my favorite station, KKBT—The Beat. It was a little past midnight when we passed Pennsylvania Avenue, then Sunland Avenue, and I think that's when I must have tripped the radar on a highway patrol car, because I was pretty sure that's when they got behind us. I told the press back then that I didn't hear the highway patrol at first, because of the music, but I'm pretty sure I saw them, and I told Dr. Drew that. I closed my eyes while I was talking to Dr. Drew, and I could almost see the flashing lights and hear the sound of the siren interrupting the music.

And suddenly it all came rushing back. That horrible sinking feeling when I saw those lights. I knew there would be hell to pay once I stopped. I knew what cops could do to guys when they were pissed off and I wanted to delay that moment forever. My buddy Pooh started yelling that I needed to stop. I eventually did, but the sirens and the lights had me pretty confused. I tried to be calm, even confident. I just wanted to close my eyes and make it all stop. But it was just the beginning of the worst night in my life.

There was a chopper in the air shining its spotlight, and LAPD swarming around. A lady cop told me to get on the ground, but then she walked away and the other officers started coming towards me. I pleaded with her to tell them they didn't have to hit me. That's when another officer walked over and kicked me in the head. He really got his foot into it and the thudding sound when his boot hit was really awful. I can still hear it.

At this point I think Dr. Drew realized what he had gotten me into, and the look on his face was serious as hell, but still calm. Dr. Drew said he could understand now how I must have thought I was going to die. I told him that absolutely, I not only believed I was going to die, but that it was only by the slimmest chance that I would be able to hold on. In fact, I believed that at one point I was dead and gone and willed myself to come back to life. He asked me again if the beating stays with me every day, and I said it does.

The world knows me as the guy who got beaten up by the cops. They don't know me for who I really am. I think about the beating every day, and I told him it reminded me in a very sad way that I'm a permanent part of this country's baggage. He asked me if I was pissed, and I said, "Oh hell yeah, I am, just festering pathetic anger, every damn day." That's why I didn't want to bring it up, and that's why I was in his rehab program. I've said I've moved on from that beating a hundred times, and every time I meant it. But there's a part that remains with me no matter what I do.

I could not give a damn, in the least, about being on TV again, or the whole celebrity factor. I told him I just wanted to try to be myself, to find myself, and save my soul. I wanted to be sane and calm again, to be happy.

Dr. Drew told me he was sorry for how I was treated and that I didn't deserve it. It felt good to hear that. I know it sounds kind of obvious, but I never get tired of hearing that I didn't deserve what those police did to me, especially from somebody I respect. And I've heard that spoken now from preachers and presidents. I was speeding, I was drinking, so let's kill the nigger. Anybody who spends two minutes with me knows who I really am, he said. Drugs knocked me down, alcohol knocked me down, and it was up to me and no one else to get up again. Dr. Drew later made a pretty big point when he told the camera that I had to deal with the beating and completely process it or else I'd start using again. That was a tough thought to get past, but I did. I knew he was right, and I knew I had to use the brutal truth of that fact to power through and beat my addiction to alcohol.

BACK TO THE BEATING

The entire group continued through rehab, each making progress in their own painful, plodding way. At one point during the second week, Dr. Drew approached me about helping him by being a leader in the group. He said I had been a quiet but consistent, lead-by-example force. This meant the world to me because it told me that all those painful evenings during withdrawal spent privately sucking it up and not whining about the night sweats, the nausea, and the recurring headaches had made a good impression on him. He was looking for a continued positive presence, someone who could intervene when others needed a role model.

I was up for anything I could do to assist Dr. Drew. He had singled me out and made it known he was proud of my attitude and effort. I've always liked going with my instincts, and that meant approaching the toughest moments of withdrawal like an athlete with a serious injury. It did no good to bitch about it, or point out how severe it was and how much I was hurting. In fact, the more I made light of it, and just gutted it out, the easier it was for me to heal up.

On day fourteen, Dr. Drew took me aside and brought up the beating again. He just wasn't going to let it alone. He was upbeat and believed he had made some headway with me when it came to me beginning to process through the whole painful event and my ordeal to get clean. He wanted to continue by having me revisit the site of the beating in hopes that it would give me closure.

Dr. Drew took me out, and we drove on the 210 freeway to where the chase started. I related what happened as best as I could. We drove to the exit I had taken that night, and we stopped on the shoulder where I had finally stopped. There was a speed limit sign there, and it was the exact same sign from that night. We walked over to the spot where the beating took place back on March 3, 1991. I looked around and just took everything in. It was a day that couldn't decide whether it wanted to be cloudy or sunny, and I remember feeling kind of hazy myself about whatever we were planning to do next. But Dr. Drew kept saying this was a good way to get closure on the whole ordeal, and I definitely felt that seventeen years was a long enough time to be tormented and unresolved. I had been to this spot before, but this was the first time I felt like I could really get something out of it.

If getting closure over this chapter in my life really meant, as Dr. Drew insisted, lasting sobriety, then I could finally cope with my reasons for standing over that cursed spot one more time. As we lingered there for a few moments, all the conflicting feelings inside me, all that rage kind of took a breath, quieted down enough for me to ask: "Okay, Rodney, now what are you going to do here? Not for the cameras, but for yourself . . . make this true, make this count."

There happened to be a helicopter flying above us right then, and it reminded me of the chopper above me that night, that the police used to light up the whole scene. I pointed out the balcony across the street where Holliday videotaped the incident. I looked at the Bible and the white flowers that we'd brought with us, and I gripped that book real tight in my right hand. I started breathing a little harder, and I couldn't seem to recall one damn clear memory of what happened that night. Then I got that tight feeling in my chest again. But this time, it was gone as fast as it came, and I was left with this amazing calm that came over me as I realized that closure was really about the future, not the past. It was about me being excited about what I could do yet with my life. Right then, and I swear this is true, the sun broke through the clouds.

I had what I called a forgiveness letter with me. I'd written it to get a lot of things off my chest that I'd been hauling around for years. I said I forgave the officers but I hadn't forgotten what happened. I realized right then and there that a part of me had already moved on. The cops got to live with what they did, and I got to do the same. What took place that night caused me a lot of stress, and it led me to do stupid things, including a lot of self-abuse through drinking.

I read my letter out loud: "This letter is to thank God for another day of life and to let some things that's been bothering me go so I can go on with my life. I need to forgive the officers who beat me the way that they did because being angry with them is not helping me. The police officers that did that to me must have personal problems, and all I can do is forgive them and put them in my prayers."

IN MEMORY OF RIOT VICTIMS

When I prayed for the people who hurt me, it helped me out mentally. I placed the letter, the flowers, and the Bible at the site. I did it in memory of the people who died in the riots. I prayed for peace for everyone. Dr. Drew said he hoped I would be able to walk away and leave this behind me. He cut right through to the core when he said that included my resentment because that's what was making me drink.

I said it felt so much better to forgive instead of walking around with a chip on my shoulder. All that hate inside me just got heavier and heavier. I know I was lucky to be alive and to be able to make this offering of my forgiveness. Dr. Drew called me an inspiration to people. He later said to the camera that maybe I'd "come to see that, at least in part, this awful experience is part of the carnage that comes with the disease of addiction."

GRADUATION

Finally, it was time for us to graduate. I got emotional standing up there and listening to the others say what they thought of me. Steven called me an "inspiration" for enduring what happened in my life. Gary, who did a lot to agitate the group in the beginning, said something really nice. People have made a joke out of my "why can't we all get along" comment during the L.A. riots, but Gary didn't think it was funny at all. He thought seriously about what I had said and took those words to heart. He even took it a step further and asked: why can't we all just get along with ourselves so we can use who we are to help others? I gave some parting words about what a great experience I'd had in rehab with this group of people. I was grateful I had a chance to try to put the puzzle of my life back together. I thanked Dr. Drew. We had a ceremony, and each of us got a coin to remind us of the journey we had been through.

When it was my turn to stand up in front of everyone, Dr. Drew thanked me for being his "go-to" man, for taking direction, and for having a good spirit and an overall positive attitude. In all honesty, there was a part of me that wished I could have stayed longer, and another part that could not wait to get out.

SOBER LIVING

Towards the end of the second VH1 show I was on, *Sober Living*, Dr. Drew wanted to discuss my plans for life and work after I left. I said I'd call my brother about a construction job. I was also thinking about moving into an apartment with my girlfriend at the time and turning the home I owned into a *Sober Living* house. It would be my way of giving back, my way of paying it forward.

I drove to my house so I could do some serious thinking about my plan. When I opened the door, I was completely shocked at what a mess the place was. It looked totally trashed. There was stuff everywhere. There was a toilet seat out back and an empty pool with gunk in it. I couldn't believe my drinking had gotten so bad that I had been living this way. I realized that my addiction had robbed me of everything. I immediately realized I couldn't set up a *Sober Living* house here. The place looked so bad, it made me think about starting to drink again. I honestly did not want to stay in my own home another day.

Dr. Drew heard about the condition of my house. He knew I would relapse if I left *Sober Living* and wasn't able to move forward with some constructive plan, so he helped me out by getting a renovation expert to redo my entire house. That way, I'd have the foundation to set up my own *Sober Living* house. The renovation guy was shocked when he saw what a wreck my place was. He had to clean, refurbish, and pretty much work all his magic in only three days.

When I arrived to see the finished work on the house, I was stunned, and became very emotional. The place was suddenly beautiful. Everything was neat and clean, and it all looked so good. It had been a long time since I'd walked into that house and seen it like it was supposed to be. They had taken some precious photos of me with my mom and of my family, framed them, and put them up on the wall. The house didn't just look like some generic fixer. They gave it a personal loving touch, and that's what meant the most to me. I hugged Dr. Drew more than once. I was really overwhelmed with the kindness.

I knew this was a brand-new start for me and I had to stay sober. This was probably the first time in my life that I was able to say those words and mean it. The reason was that Dr. Drew had put his faith in me with his actions and not just words. He had gone that extra mile and done a magnificent job of fixing up my home so that I could steady myself and pay it all forward. Here was someone who was willing to back up his belief in my sobriety with this amazingly selfless effort. This wasn't just lip service, and it touched me very deeply.

Now if I could clean up the mess that was my life the way Dr. Drew had done with the house, then my future could be full of promise. Staying sober was the least I could do to thank him, or as the doctor would be quick to correct me, the least I could do to thank myself.

Overall, my experience on *Celebrity Rehab* and the spin-off, *Sober House,* was okay. It made me look at the whole process in a different light. I enjoyed meeting all those people, because we did feel like family at times, and it made me realize that having that kind of support does make getting clean and sober more achievable.

I might have thought that since I had finally gotten clean in a way that was more appealing to me, it was more likely to last, more likely to stick. But that would prove not to be the case.

But as I sat down in my now beautiful living room, I had every reason to be hopeful that getting clean was the crucial step to a better life. I even said a little prayer of thanks because I really believed that by taking it a day at a time, it would all be fine.

Chapter 9

LIVE, LEARN, LOVE

A BETTER WORLD

There has been a lot written over the last twenty years about how the Rodney King incident has left our country a less safe place to live. Books and magazines churned out claims that law enforcement officers had been forced to be excessively timid in dealing with situations where a dangerous suspect offers resistance to arrest. The police had been ever mindful that two of the officers who beat me were sent to jail and lost their pensions and livelihood after appearing in federal court to account for the alleged racially motivated excessive force they displayed on the night of my beating.

There is no doubt, they insisted, that neighborhoods had been left less safe and that police officers were more vulnerable to bodily injury because they were no longer willing to use the proper tactics to ensure their safety while securing the suspect's arrest. Fear of being held accountable for any act that may be labeled police brutality, or excessive force, left us with law enforcement that was meek and ineffective.

If that was the case, then I have one thing to say: I am sincerely sorry. I apologize if the violation of my civil rights has made us less safe. That was never my intention or the objective of the lawyers that represented me. Looking back, I deserved to be arrested that night. I was drinking and I was speeding and I was breaking the law. Anyone clocked at over 100 mph on the highway and topping 60 mph on surface streets deserves to be pulled over because they are a clear menace to themselves and the lives of others. I saw the lights from the police cruiser, and I knew that as soon as I refused to pull over, I was going to be charged with offenses far worse than speeding. I was drinking and my judgment that night was certainly impaired, but that's no excuse for refusing to pull over. It was beyond stupid and it was dangerous and it was wrong.

But the LAPD wanted me to believe that what happened next was not racially motivated. I've wanted to accept that, because so much of the positive message I want to spread, so much of the forgiveness that I worked on with Dr. Drew and many others, is based on that. Just because I was black and those cops were white didn't mean they were more motivated to pull me over and order me out of that white Hyundai. The second they shined that flashlight into my car was the moment, however, when they discovered I was a young black male with two black male passengers. Only the four officers that beat me can account for their actions by telling us what they were really thinking and why they did what they did. My closure stood separate and independent of their thoughts and deeds. They can quote protocol and their "fear factor" and all their other babble until Judgment Day, but they must come clean and tell the truth about what they were really thinking. If they have, then praise the Lord, and if they haven't, then that is their burden and no one else's.

Over the years, "Rodney King" has become synonymous with drinking, DUIs, domestic violence, reckless driving, civil rights violations, police brutality, hate crimes—the list goes on and on. Any random day, Google Alerts yields at least half a dozen reports, blogs, and reader comments on sites like *The Huffington Post* and *The Independent*. Here are just a few results from a Google Alert for my name:

Brooke Fantelli, California Transgender Woman, Allegedly Tased in the Crotch by Imperial County Desert Rangers
The Huffington Post

"I don't call it a huge case of police brutality because compared to black Americans like **Rodney King**, I mean that is police brutality to the worst case. Police use brute force because that is what they are trained to use, and that is part of the . . ."

Pivotal Week for Economic Stimulus Resolution
The Root

In the words of **Rodney King**. . . Seriously, this fighting and tugging while leaving the country in a lurch is not cool.

Henry Louis Gates at Politics & Prose
Washington City Paper

So, it's understandable if reading about the Middle Passage, post-Civil War Reconstruction, and the **Rodney King** riots might get exhausting.

America Needs Us, Mr. President
The Independent

I used to say, ". . . But if you end up on the **Rodney King** tape, I will write that." Now they tell me about their mistakes. They would never do that when I was a reporter.

Rapper T. I. Tells *Vibe* Some Gay People Are Acting Un-American when Rallying against Anti-Gay Comments
The Huffington Post

I think his statement is akin to the old saw "let us agree to disagree." Right now I could use some of that vintage philosophy from **Rodney King**: "Can't we all just get along?"

Occutards Gonna Occutard: Black Friday Edition
Economics Job Market Rumors

God, these dumbfucks make me long for the days of police brutality. They all need to be **Rodney King**'d.

Rodney King'd? So now I've even become a verb, but when will I become a real person, a whole person? None of this makes me do anything more than shake my head. If I tried to keep track of what I've influenced and who I've inspired, shocked, disgusted, or disappointed, I'd never leave the house, and that can't happen because I still love being outdoors all day long.

GETTING RODNEY'D

Outdoors or indoors, come evening, my fiancé and I love catching a movie. We just saw an excellent new film titled

Rampart starring Woody Harrelson as a corrupt LAPD cop. This might be Woody's best film ever. He is totally convincing as a corrupt, down-on-his-luck Los Angeles police officer. Harrelson is caught, in the decade after my beating, pummeling a suspect with his baton in broad daylight after a traffic accident. The suspect/driver of the car T-bones the black-and-white that Harrelson is driving while on duty. After Harrelson's air bag deploys, he gathers himself, gets out of his cruiser and, already furious, confronts the driver, still sitting in his car. But as he is about to get in the driver's face, the suspect suddenly, as if rehearsed, opens his car door and slams it into Harrelson, completely surprising him. This buys him time to take off running up a grassy patch next to the road. But Harrelson catches up to him, knocks him down, and commences, in a completely uncontrolled rage, to beat the hell out of him.

Now, this was a very interesting scene for me to watch, because of my reaction. I was rooting for Woody to pound the hell out of the asshole who was driving so recklessly. Then I kind of caught myself when I figured out that was me! I was the one guy in America who might feel differently about what he was seeing, and who he was rooting for, on the screen. But I didn't—the guy was a jerk and deserved a good beating. For the first time in my life, I might have caught an inkling of how Powell, Briseno, Wind, and Koon felt that night. Damn.

In the film, someone captures Woody's abuse with a video camera or whatever, and Harrelson becomes the lead story on the evening news. His superiors are upset with him and threaten to have him reviewed and tossed off the force. But one of his bosses, a character played by Steve Buscemi, says something that everyone is thinking: this officer was responding to the call of duty, and the only thing he did wrong was get caught on camera. I caught myself understanding that, seeing it the cop's way.

RAPPING THE TRUTH

When it comes to movies, my life, and my beliefs, one of my all-time favorite movie scenes is from a Halle Berry movie called *Bulworth*. Warren Beatty plays a U.S. senator being interviewed on a TV news show. It is one of the most brilliant performances in the history of cinema. He launches into a spontaneous, hilarious rap in front of a female news anchor and rips apart the hypocrisy of politics, our government, and the way our leaders are corrupted by big business and the system.

Senator Bulworth appears on the TV news show because he is campaigning for reelection. Instead of his usual suit and tie, he is dressed in rapper clothes and SweptBack sunglasses, much to the confusion and curiosity of the interviewer, who happens to ask him something about obscenity. Bulworth launches into this incredible rap, which ends with him basically saying what I said in an earlier chapter: if we all just keep making love to one another without regard to race, soon there won't be any race, because we'll all look the same.

I cracked up when the camera cut to an elderly black woman with her family watching Bulworth rap on TV from her living room across town. All she says is, "Damn!"

Damn is right. Damn right.

People just need to hear the truth. For me, Dr. Drew was the truth. I may not have wanted to hear it, but I responded to it. I went towards it, even though I went kicking and screaming. I was drawn to it—we are all drawn to the truth. We get nowhere by ignoring how bad things are or how tough it will be to make them better. We need somebody to just say it like it is, even if it hurts. The worst parts of my life were when I wasn't being honest with myself. Living lies gets you nowhere.

HOW FAR WE'VE GOT TO GO

It's November 22, 2011, and we're working on the final chapter of my memoirs. A morning paper is sitting on the counter of the place where I get my coffee. I order smokes and flip through it while the guy behind the counter goes in the back to crack open a fresh carton of Newports for me. It's a beautiful sunny day in Southern California, a little on the cool side, which is fine this time of year. Like a lot of Americans, I always think of President Kennedy on this day. Being a lover of history and a total History Channel geek, that night I check to see if there is anything on TV—movie, special, or documentary—about JFK.

It's hard to believe that his death, something that happened two years before I was born, is now two years away from its fiftieth anniversary. My parents used to talk about how much they loved President Kennedy and how his assassination, along with his brother Bobby Kennedy's and Martin Luther King Jr.'s, were terrible tragedies and major setbacks for Civil Rights and black Americans.

Most of the headlines I saw on TV on the twenty-second were still about the pepper spraying of a thousand seated students at UC Davis and the chancellor of the school's speech. "I am here to apologize," Linda Katehi said. "I feel horrible for what happened." But the crowd reaction was mixed with boos and cries of "Let her speak!" The whole incident was captured on videos that quickly went viral on the Internet, infinitely faster than my beating video circulated the nation. In fact, the video of the police officers spraying the students with pepper spray already has over a million and a half hits on YouTube.

If it is anything that has to do with excessive abuse or police brutality, you can bet my name is going to come up. And there it is on the Google Alert: "According to MSNBC's Ed Schultz, the pepper-spraying of UC Davis students who refused to disperse is equivalent to the Rodney King beating." Schultz channeled his sixties hippy self when he called the police "pigs," while comparing them to the cops who beat me in the 1990s. Said Schultz:

"I equate this to the Rodney King beating. I really do. The action's no different than taking a nightstick out on a guy or to go right up and pepper spray people right in the face when they're absolutely harmless. What's the difference?" he asked. A ten-minute video reveals that student protesters basically gave their permission to be pepper sprayed. This was in spite of the fact that police allowed the protesters plenty of time to leave the area.

The MSNBC spokesman claimed that the media neglected to run the segment of video showing the cops patiently encouraging the protesters to leave. I was surprised that Schultz didn't pick up on the fact that my video was also edited, shortened by the media.

The unedited video would have told a different story. That is why the officers testified at the Simi Valley hearing that they feared for their lives. The first seven seconds of my video, which was not included in the evening news broadcasts, showed me getting up and running. I was trying to run away. The court allowed that that might have been the case, or I may have been running towards a cop. But all these comparisons don't seem to benefit anyone. They don't teach us a thing except to remind us that we are repeating the same mistakes, that the only thing learned from history is that we are helpless to repeat it.

It never stops. And if I'm just being matched up with another case of abuse, how is that helping? It just proves that we haven't learned from it, benefited because of it, or improved on it at all.

After the pepper spray story, I watched the follow-up to the Brandon McInerney case. McInerney avoided a retrial by an outright guilty plea to shooting Larry King. The jury deadlocked in the first trial after the 2008 shooting, with some saying prosecutors were being too harsh in trying Brandon as an adult.

McInerney was a teenager who fatally shot a gay classmate in the back of the head in an Oxnard, California, middle school computer lab. He will spend twenty-one years in prison under the plea deal reached November 21, 2011. The case drew international headlines and a debate on how schools should handle sexual identity issues.

McInerney was fourteen when he pulled a gun out of his backpack and shot Larry King two times at point-blank range. He will be behind bars until he is thirty-eight under the terms of the deal struck by Ventura County prosecutors. In an unusual arrangement, the seventeen-year-old pleaded guilty to second-degree and voluntary manslaughter. In return, prosecutors agreed not to go forward with a second trial, which could have resulted in a life sentence. The family of the victim, Larry King, broke their silence on the case outside court, saying that they supported the sentence but believed school officials hold deep responsibility for what happened.

"Larry had a complicated life, but he did not deserve to be murdered," said the youth's father, Greg King. But the saddest comment came from the mother of King, who revealed for the first time that she had contacted school officials four days before the shooting in an effort to solicit their cooperation in toning down her son's behavior. The boy had been taken from the Kings' house two months earlier by authorities because of problems at home. She said she was told that her son had a civil right to explore his sexual identity.

"I knew, gut instinct, that something serious was going to happen," King's mother said. "They should have contained him, contained his behavior."

Was it their fault? With these kinds of tragedies, it's always the same answer: yes and no.

But the thing I find so frustrating about these front-page stories is the fact that we're not moving forward, as a race of people, towards a more peaceful path of tolerance and understanding. We're just as close-minded and violent as we were twenty years ago when I was brutally beaten and Tasered by police. We're just as prejudiced and poisoned by hate as we were when my gay teacher friend, Mr. Jones, was shot and killed by a vengeful student from John Muir High School. What have we learned? What have we changed? How have we improved? In both cases, a gay male lay dead from bullet wounds. Larry King's only crime was that he was an admitted homosexual.

CHILDREN ARE THE KEY

Now, I have given this one revelation I had a lot of consideration. And it came after I was asked what I recommend when it comes to us building a less racist, more peace-loving world. The initial idea just kind of sprung up from my gut, and then I had to think it through so that people could understand what it is I'm proposing. Let's start with the idea that everyone on earth can agree on one thing: we love our children. If we begin with this undeniable truth, then it isn't too big a leap to agree we want a better future for our children.

Well, I want to go a step further and say that children are the key to that better tomorrow. They are our opportunity because young kids are so pure, they are color-blind by nature.

I say we should take advantage of that and make sure our children are thoroughly integrated starting at the youngest possible age. Let all youngsters spend more time with each other, in day care, in preschool, in every activity whether it be sports, summer camp, at the playground, birthday parties, sleepovers, lunch rooms, or living rooms. The sooner and longer our children are mixing it up with each other, the better we will all get along.

Why? Because I am hoping our children will be amused to discover that there are grown-ups out there who make a big deal over our appearance. Let our children realize that such emphasis on the differences in our looks is just plain stupid. Tricia is white, Louie is yellow, and Lisa is black, but so what? And let their parents laugh with them, and show their kids they are wise and tolerant in a world sorely in need of more wisdom and tolerance.

Then we can all laugh at the racists who try to create bad feelings between kids who have different colored skin, different hair, and different shape of eyes. I believe that is our best chance for a more peaceful planet. And I think if we start right now, we can achieve this in our children's children's lifetimes.

REDEMPTION

The saddest day in creation for me was after the swimming hole incident, when I realized I was no longer just a kid, I was a black kid. I'd like to find a way of forever removing that day from every black child's life. I'm sure that for some children with loving parents, it is a moment of profound pride. But for too many, it is still a time of confusion and mixed emotions.

Redemption for me is a hard-fought desire that comes in small doses, little moments when I can show a black kid and a white kid how to field a hard-hit grounder to third base. When I can be with my daughter and her friends and make them laugh.

The riot within me has not been purged, only controlled, minimized. I would love to say I am hate free, completely reborn into love for all my fellow human beings. I have not experienced a divine moment of total forgiveness or benefited from some blessed revelation that allowed me to forgive and forget the past. But I have found peace in my grandchild's smile, my fiancé's embrace, my family's laughter. I have never had a better relationship with my mother nor a healthier one with the rest of my family.

There were no trumpet blasts or national talk shows announcing my sudden enlightenment. Each day is a struggle, each day a battle to find serenity and purpose. But I now approach the ways to redemption as opportunities for positive feelings, and not some begrudging step on the way to clarity and sobriety. When I resisted Dr. Drew's attempts to bring up the beating so I could obtain some closure and move toward a foundation for my sobriety, I still felt like the pain of recalling that night would overshadow any attempt to forgive and feel better. But again with the small steps. Dr. Drew got me to the site with flowers and a Bible, and I discovered that closure is about the future, not the past.

A reporter from the *New York Times* once came to interview me at my house. I explained to him how I would like to be remembered. "I don't want to be remembered as the person who started the riots. I'd like to be remembered for the person who threw water on the whole thing. Part of the solution, you know? I want to be remembered as the person who tried to keep peace in this country, that I did my part."

I am not totally clean, I have not completely forgotten, I am not without misgivings, but I want to be. I sincerely want to be a better human being. There is no longer a riot raging within me. I have forgiven the politicians and lawyers who tried so hard to make me what I was not. I no longer blame them for taking a battered and confused addict and trying to make him into a symbol for civil rights. I realize I will always be the poster child for police brutality, but I can try to use that as a positive force for healing and restraint.

My heart is in the right place, my mind is optimistic about the future, and my spirit is alive and hopeful. There is much work ahead for me, but I have surrounded myself with people who are not toxic, who truly love me and want the best for me. I've discovered that redemption is best kept within reach and is often attained just as surely by the things I choose not to do. By striving for redemption, I can seek the good that moves me in the right direction.

I've thought a lot about my dad while writing my memoirs and have dedicated myself to what he taught me as a child. He said we should all be positive and happy, be the type of person others look forward to being around. Be likeable, smile, don't let their prejudices cast shadows across your life. Show them how prejudicial actions and beliefs only hurt us all, and that anyone who is truly trying to be a better person has to do away with that toxic behavior first.

I may slip again, but Rodney Glen King will never stop trying to be a better person—creaky bones, headaches, and all. We all have a dream, and mine is to take all God's children down to the fishing hole, soak in the sun, and savor the beautiful colors in creation that He has given us, like a rainbow trout.

MY FAMILY, MY FUTURE. MY LETTER TO YOU . . .

I've been asked, "Why a book, Rodney?" and with just as much curiosity, "Why now?"

Fact is, I've tried more than once over the last twenty years to write about my life experience and what happened to me at the hands of the police and our system of justice. I've really wanted to do it at times, but during other periods I wasn't sure if I really had a good enough reason to pull it all together. Regardless of my desire, the pages never quite seemed like they came from me and the way I like to communicate with people. I knew I needed to dig deep to get readers to experience what it was really like to be there and how it felt, in the aftermath, to rebuild a shattered body and mind.

Even when I go back over certain sections of this book, like the one on the beating, I still feel like I've barely touched on the trauma and evil of that experience. When I tell you that my clothes were soaked in blood, or that I heard my bones crack, it does not do justice to the pain and utter despair I went through.

For many years I felt that I had been involuntarily burdened as the victim and resultant universal symbol of Police Brutality. I wanted no part of it, just wanted to stay home, drink and watch TV. Recalling the past only filled me with fear or rage. There was an element of my personal pride that had been permanently destroyed as a result of the beating. No man could possibly relish the thought of there being a video in existence of him having the crap beat out of him. The fact that this footage was sent out to be viewed by the entire world certainly didn't help with my recovery. It was completely humiliating to me, and to my friends and family.

But during the last couple of years, I have finally gotten some traction back into my life. It started with a period of serious sobriety, courtesy of Dr. Drew. I realize that there is a greater purpose to be discovered in each person's life—even when it's not that apparent. Sometimes I grasp this at the oddest times, like when I make myself help my brother Gailen in spite of the fact that I don't feel like it. He has been through so much, and I believe the good Lord has put him here to show me that I am fortunate in many ways. Gailen is a part of my family, which has always been a source of wisdom and strength for me.

As I get older, and hopefully a little wiser, I realize that in the end it's all about family. As I think back on my life, it's family I treasure the most. My father had a rough life, but always managed a big smile and a pleasant attitude around his bosses. I think of how hard that must have been for him, but he did it because he had to hold down two thankless jobs to feed and shelter us. My mother has always been a blessed presence, juggling the impossible, holding down a job cleaning houses while raising a large family. She embraced her God as a Jehovah's Witness, leading by example, a devoutly religious woman who carried her crosses with quiet dignity. My brothers and sisters are my life, guardians and confidants. Each is so different yet so much alike. We went through heaven and hell as youngsters, and each of us has had our fair share of struggles as adults, but we have always been there for each other.

Lately I've thought more and more about the love I have for my own three daughters, and now my two grandchildren! Nothing makes a man more aware of his responsibilities and blessings than his children. We see ourselves in their eyes, in their mannerisms, their speech, humor and laughter. I know each of them will struggle in their own way, but I want them to know now more than ever that I am here to lighten their burden, and that together we can get through anything.

I saw an article recently from Kerry Egan, a hospice chaplain in Massachusetts. It was a very enlightening and inspirational piece. She wrote that in their final days, people mostly talk about their families, about their mothers and fathers, their sons and daughters. When we talk about our families, Kerry realized, that is the way we talk about God. She goes on to say that we don't learn the meaning of our lives in books, lecture halls, churches, synagogues, or mosques. No, the meaning of our lives is discovered through actions of love. And if God is love, then we learn about God when we learn about love. Kerry points out that the first and last classroom of love is the family. Like me, she is amazed at the strength of the human soul. I got chills when I realized that it was my soul that survived the night of the beating, stubbornly pulling my mind and body along with it. Why? Because it was not my time, because there was something worthwhile and good for me to do on this earth. Otherwise I would have died that night.

For me, the most important part of Kerry's writing was

when she pointed out that when the love is imperfect, like when a family is flawed or destructive, something else is learned, and that is forgiveness. The spiritual work of being human is learning how to love and how to forgive. I firmly believe that's true, and it may be the most important thing we can learn from living. Family is the most powerful force in this world. It reminds me I'm not alone, that I truly belong to something real and beautiful. I took pride in that, even when I messed up over the years.

When people read this book, I hope they realize that no matter how bad it gets, they are never alone. Whatever problems we have, and whatever terrible things happen to us, we can rise above them. We may be scarred, and we may not be able to forget, but we can keep going, one step at a time, until we get to a better place.

My life has been about my immortal soul from the start, and now that my spirit is mostly healed, I can begin a new journey lit by forgiveness and love. That's why today, this moment, I believe I have arrived at that better place in mind, body, and soul. And I guess that's why this was the best time for me to write it all down.

It's now time for me to try to reach out and help others get to their better place. By letting go of the Riot Within, by telling my story truly and honestly, I have been able to heal. And if someone like me can heal and find peace, then there is plenty of hope for all of us!

ACKNOWLEDGMENTS

My thanks and gratitude that this book came to life. I personally would like to thank the world for all the prayers and support through one of the most tragic days of my life. I know without a doubt that without your prayers I would not be here to share my story. An enormous thanks to HarperCollins for giving me the opportunity after twenty years to have my book come to life for the world to read about my Journey.

Can we all get along? Maybe one day.

Special thanks to:

Editor Nancy Hancock, assistant Elsa Dixon, publicist Suzanne Wickham, agents Jason Allen Ashlock and Adam Chromy, Tom Swift, and Sam and Kathy Spagnola.

BIBLIOGRAPHY

BIBLIOGRAPHY A: PRE-RIOTS; FEDERAL TRIAL; CELEBRITY REHAB

1989 Conviction

Associated Press. "Grocer Testifies King Lied About 1989 Robbery." *Chicago Tribune*. April 6, 1994, North Sports final edition.

Deutsch, Linda. "King Says He's Not Guilty of Robbery Count on His Record." *Los Angeles Times*. March 31, 1994, Southland edition.

Dunn, Ashley, and Andrea Ford. "L.A. Beating Victim Called Ordinary Guy / Even Grocer He Robbed in 1989 Says King Didn't Have the Heart to Hurt Him." *San Francisco Chronicle*. March 16, 1991, final edition.

———. "The Man Swept Up in the Furor: Friends, Family Say King Was Sometimes Lost but Never Violent." *Los Angeles Times*. March 17, 1991.

Stevenson, Richard W. "Tape Forever Ties Victim to Beating." *New York Times*. March 20, 1991.

Thompson, Elise. "Rodney King Forgives Officers Who Beat Him." *LAist*. February 22, 2009. http://laist.com/2009/02/22/rodney_king_forgives.php.

Trial/Police Acquittal/L.A. Riots

Cannon, Lou. "'There Was No Reason' to Beat Rodney King, Officer Testifies." *Houston Chronicle*. March 7, 1992, Two Star edition.

Gates, Daryl F. "L.A.P.D. Chief in Rodney King Era, Dies at 83." *New York Times*. April 16, 2010.

LeDuff, Charlie. "12 Years After the Riots, Rodney King Gets Along." *New York Times*. September 19, 2004.

Los Angeles Times. "The Rodney King Affair." March 24, 1991, home edition.

Mitchell, John L., and Tina Daunt. "King Jury's Voice of Reason Carried a Private Burden." *Los Angeles Times*. June 3, 1994. http://articles.latimes.com/1994-06-03/news/mn-65530_1_jury-room/2.

Mydans, Seth. "The Police Verdict; Los Angeles Policemen Acquitted in Taped Beating." *New York Times.* April 30, 1992.

San Francisco Chronicle. "Cop's Remarks Ruled Racist and Relevant / Setback for Defense in Rodney King Case." June 11, 1991.

———. "Officers Acquitted in Videotaped Rodney King Beating." April 30, 1992, final edition.

———. "Prosecution Rests in Rodney King Case / Deputy D.A. Decides Not to Have Victim of Police Beating Testify." March 18, 1992, final edition.

Viacom International Inc. *Celebrity Rehab 2 with Dr. Drew.* 2008. http://www.vh1.com/shows/celebrity_rehab_with_dr_drew/season_2/series.jhtml.

Wood, Daniel. "Chronology of the Rodney King Case." *The Christian Science Monitor* (Boston, MA). May 12, 1992.

Civil Rights Lawsuit

All Things Considered. "Jury Denies King Any Damages from Police Officers." National Public Radio. June 1, 1994.

Associated Press. "L.A. OKs $3.8 Million for Rodney King." *Chicago Tribune.* August 4, 1994, North Sports final edition.

———. "L.A., Rodney King End Legal Fight; City to Pay $3.8 Million." *Denver Post.* August 4, 1994.

Hamilton, William. "King Is Awarded $3.8 Million in L.A. Police Beating." *The Washington Post.* April 20, 1994, final edition.

Larsen, Peter. "King Gets $3.8 Million in '91 L.A. Beating." *Pittsburgh Post-Gazette.* April 20, 1994.

Los Angeles Times. "Council OKs Plan to Set Aside $2 Million for King." *Los Angeles Times.* August 10, 1994, home edition.

Mitchell, John L. "Punitive Damages from Police in King Beating Rejected in Courts." *Los Angeles Times.* June 2, 1994, home edition.

Morning Edition. "Laurence Powell Takes Stand in Rodney King Criminal Trial." National Public Radio. April 26, 1994.

Mydans, Seth. "May 29–June 4: Endless Trials; Jurors Decide Against Assessing More Damages." *New York Times.* June 5, 1994.

———. "Jury Sets King's Award L.A. Beating Victim to Get $3.8 Million." *Denver Post.* April 20, 1994, Rockies edition.

———. "King Wins $3.8 Million in Damages/L.A. Told to Pay Over '91 Beating." *Houston Chronicle.* April 20, 1994, Two Star edition.

Rainey, James, and Richard A. Serrano. "L.A. Considers Record Payment in King Suit Police." *Los Angeles Times*. June 25, 1992, home edition.

San Francisco Chronicle. "King Case Expert Called Too Depressed to Testify." April 28, 1994, Three Star edition.

———. "Rodney King Gets $3.8 Million in First Phase of Lawsuit." April 20, 1994, final edition.

Serrano, Richard. "3 in King Beating Say They Feared for Lives," *Los Angeles Times*. May 21, 1991.

Skowron, Sandra. "King Lawyers Reject Offer of $1 Million." *Los Angeles Sentinel*. July 16, 1994, home edition.

Post-Beating Rap

CBSNews. "Rodney King Pleads Not Guilty to DUI Charges." November 8, 2011. http://www.cbsnews.com/8301-504083_162-57320480-504083/rodney-king-pleads-not-guilty-to-dui-charge/

Chicago Tribune. "Rodney King Out on Bail After DUI Arrest." July 13, 2011. http://amren.com/oldnews/archives/2011/07/rodney_king_out.php.

———. "Rodney King Faces a DUI Charge." May 22, 1995, evening update, C edition.

Leibowitz, Ed. "Rodney's Rap." *Los Angeles Times*. March 28, 1999, home edition.

Los Angeles Times. "Rodney King Acquitted in Pennsylvania DUI Case." March 30, 1996, home edition.

———. "Rodney King Pleads Not Guilty to Spousal Abuse Charges." October 21, 1995, home edition.

———. "Trial Set for Rodney King in Assault, Spousal Abuse Case." January 26, 1996, home edition.

———. "Wife Recounts Incident with King." July 4, 1996, home edition.

McClatchy–Tribune Business News (Washington, DC). "Rodney King Charged with DUI for July Arrest." August 24, 2011. http://www.mspnews.com/news/2011/08/25/5729971.htm

Rainey, James. "A Man of Conflicting Images." *Los Angeles Times*. August 3, 1995, home edition.

Reston, Maeve. "Rodney King Shot While Riding Bike." *Los Angeles Times*. November 30, 2007.

Saar, Mayrav. "After Mixed Verdict, King Looks to the Future." *Los Angeles Times*. July 12, 1996, home edition.

San Francisco Chronicle. "Rodney King Freed on Bail / Domestic Abuse, Assault Investigation." July 17, 1995, final edition.

Tribune News Services. "Rodney King Is Charged with Abuse." *Chicago Tribune.* March 6, 1999, Chicagoland final edition.

Federal Trial

Andrews, James H. "US Justice Is on Trial in Rodney King Case." *The Christian Science Monitor* (Boston, MA). March 15, 1993.

Cannon, Lou. "Prosecutors in Beating Trial Seen as Making Better Case This Time; Observers Cite Strong Law Enforcement and Medical Witnesses." *The Washington Post.* March 15, 1993, final edition.

Connelly, Michael. "Legal Motions Further Split King Defendants." *Los Angeles Times.* October 6, 1992, Southland edition.

Deutsch, Linda. "Policemen Surrender for Trial in King Case." *The Independent.* August 7, 1992.

———. "4 L.A. Officers Appear in Court, Post Bail on Civil Rights Charges." *Philadelphia Inquirer.* August 7, 1992.

Greenhouse, Linda. "Court Upholds Sentence in King Case." *New York Times.* June 14, 1996.

Holding, Reynolds. "Federal Civil Rights Prosecutions / Unrealistic Hopes After King Verdict." *San Francisco Chronicle.* April 23, 1993, final edition.

Morning Edition. "Civil Rights Charges Against King Beaters." National Public Radio. August 6, 1992.

Nelson, Jack. "Bush Denounces Rioting in L.A. as 'Purely Criminal.'" *Los Angeles Times.* May 1, 1992, home edition.

Newton, Jim. "Beaten King Was 'Shown Off' by 2 Officers, Jury Told." *Los Angeles Times.* February 26, 1993, home edition.

———. "Koon, Powell Get 2 1/2 Years in Prison Anger, Unease Greet Decision; Appeals Seen Likely." *Los Angeles Times.* August 5, 1993, home edition.

Newton, Jim, and Henry Weinstein. "Court Orders Longer Sentences for Koon, Powell." *Los Angeles Times.* August 20, 1994, home edition.

Rosenthal, Harry F. "13 Dead in L.A. Rioting." *Orange County Register.* April 30, 1992.

Stewart, Sally Ann. "What Did I Do to Deserve That Type of Pain? I Was Just Trying to Stay Alive." *USA Today.* March 10, 1993.

University of Missouri–Kansas City School of Law. "LAPD Officers' Trials: A Chronology." *Famous American Trials.* http://law2.umkc.edu/faculty/projects/ftrials/lapd/kingchronology.html.

BIBLIOGRAPHY B: RIOTS; FIRST TRIAL; APPEARANCES POST-RIOT UNTIL CELEBRITY REHAB

Adams, Guy. "Rodney King vs. The Police, Round 2." *The Independent.* September 12, 2009. http://www.youtube.com/watch?v=22s1mP1w3uE.

Becklund, Laurie, and Stephanie Chavez. "Beaten Driver a Searing Image of Mob Cruelty." May 01, 1992. http://articles.latimes.com/1992-05-01/news/mn-1393_1_truck-driver.

Burns Ortiz, Maria. "Inside the Celebrity Boxing Federation." *ESPN.* November 18, 2009. http://sports.espn.go.com/espn/page2/story?page=ortiz/091118.

Cassingham, Randy. "A Fool and His Money Are Soon Parted." *This Is True.* July 6, 1997. http://www.thisistrue.com/a_fool_and_his_money_are_soon_parted_5506.html.

Celebrity Boxing Federation. "Rodney King Interview." YouTube. Uploaded by MegaStarPro on November 13, 2009. http://www.youtube.com/watch?v=CMxJ83qjmJE&feature=related.

Chardon, Phillip. "L.A. Riots." *South Central History.* http://www.southcentralhistory.com/la-riots.php.

———. "Watts Riots." *South Central History.* http://www.southcentralhistory.com/watts-riots.php.

Chavez, Stephanie. "Trial Watchers Feed Mainly on Tidbits." *Los Angeles Times.* April 29, 1992. http://articles.latimes.com/1992-04-29/local/me-927_1_jury-room.

Clifford, Frank, and Louis Sahagun. "City Leaders Voice Helplessness as They Grope for Answers." *Los Angeles Times.* May 01, 1992. http://articles.latimes.com/1992-05-01/local/me-1523_1_power-structure.

CNN. "Race Rage: The Beating of Rodney King." YouTube. Uploaded by taritrott on March 6, 2011. http://www.youtube.com/watch?v=tWhYmb1sANM.

Corwin, Miles. "Everyday Life Shattered in Many Ways." *Los Angeles Times.* May 1, 1992. http://articles.latimes.com/1992-05-01/news/mn-1408_1_los-angeles-central-library.

El Nasser, Haya. "Rodney King's Suit Against L.A. Under Way Today." *USA Today*. March 22, 1994, final edition.

Ford, Andrea. "Crips, Bloods Have Month of No Pay-Backs." *Los Angeles Times*. May 30, 1992. http://articles.latimes.com/1992-05-30/local/me-318_1_gang-truce.

Gerstenzang, James, and Ashley Dunn. "Punish Rioters, Bush Tells L.A." *Los Angeles Times*. May 30, 1992. http://articles.latimes.com/1992-05-30/news/mn-230_1_specific-financial-aid.

Graham, Nicholas. "Rodney King to Fight Former Police Officer in 'Celebrity Boxing Match.'" *The Huffington Post*. November 10, 2009. http://www.huffingtonpost.com/2009/09/10/rodney-king-to-fight-form_n_282866.html.

Griego, Tina. "2 Cities—Under Siege and Under Threat: Compton Declares a State of Emergency as Looters Run Wild." *Los Angeles Times*. May 1, 1992. http://articles.latimes.com/1992-05-01/local/me-1516_1_city-council.

Haldane, David. "Guard Troops Drill for L.A. Riot Duty." *Los Angeles Times*. May 01, 1992. http://articles.latimes.com/1992-05-01/local/me-1309_1_gulf-war.

Haring, Bruce. "Rodney King Constructing New Career as Rap Impresario." *USA Today*.

Hartley-Parkinson, Richard. "Rodney King Pulled Over by Police Almost 20 Years to the Day Since His Arrest and Savage Beating Sparked Riots in L.A." *Daily Mail*. March 4, 2011. http://www.dailymail.co.uk/news/article-1362952/Rodney-King-arrested-skipping-red-light-20-years-LA-riots.html#ixzz1eYYNB9il.

Illouz, Eva. "Oprah Winfrey and the Glamour of Misery: An Essay on Popular Culture." New York: Columbia Univ. Press, 2003.

Kasindorf, Martin. "Few Signs of L.A. Riots Remain." *USA Today*. April 19, 2002.

KCAL. "Rare Rodney King Interview." YouTube. Uploaded by bx-cubariikan718 on March 7, 2009. http://www.youtube.com/watch?v=pmJJpOso-70&feature=related.

Lacey, Marc, and Shawn Hubler. "Rioters Set Fires, Loot Stores; 4 Reported Dead." *Los Angeles Times*. April 30, 1992. http://articles.latimes.com/1992-04-30/news/mn-1893_1_fire-department

LeDuff, Charlie. "12 Years After the Riots, Rodney King Gets Along." *New York Times.* September 19, 2004. http://www.nytimes.com/2004/09/19/national/19king.html.

Lieberman, Paul. "Post-Riot Justice Is Often Ruled by 'Luck of Draw.'" *Los Angeles Times.* May 30, 1992. http://articles.latimes.com/1992-05-30/news/mn-229_1_district-attorney.

Live Leak. "Absolutely Horrific—The Reginald Denny and Fidel Lopez Beatings." May 6, 2011. http://www.liveleak.com/view?i=1cb_1304689062.

Lopez, Robert J. "Rodney King Stopped After Traffic Violation, Police Say." *Los Angeles Times.* March 4, 2011, local edition. http://latimesblogs.latimes.com/lanow/2011/03/rodney-king-stopped.html.

Los Angeles Times. "Mapping L.A.: Historic South-Central." 2000. http://projects.latimes.com/mapping-la/neighborhoods/neighborhood/historic-south-central/.

McGuire, Stryker. "Remaking Rodney King." *Newsweek.* May 9, 1994.

Mobbmuzik. "Stranded." http://mobbmuzik.blogspot.com/2009/03/stranded-stranded-comptonca.html.

Nelson, Jack. "Bush Denounces Rioting in L.A. as 'Purely Criminal.'" *Los Angeles Times.* May 01, 1992. http://articles.latimes.com/1992-05-01/news/mn-1416_1_white-house.

News & Notes. "Dr. Drew, Rodney King Talk 'Celebrity Rehab.'" National Public Radio. October 22, 2008. http://www.npr.org/templates/story/story.php?storyId=95985967.

Pool, Bob. "People Eager to Buy Weapons Turned Away." *Los Angeles Times.* May 01, 1992. http://articles.latimes.com/1992-05-01/local/me-1520_1_los-angeles.

RadarOnline.com. "Rodney King to Marry Juror From Cop Beating Trial." September 7, 2010. http://www.radaronline.com/exclusives/2010/09/exclusive-rodney-king-marry-juror-cop-beating-trial.

Republican Newsroom, The. "Rodney King Added to Celebrity Boxing Federation Undercard Bout at Springfield Sheraton." *MassLive.* October 26, 2009. http://www.masslive.com/news/index.ssf/2009/10/rodney_king_added_to_celebrity.html.

Reston, Maeve. "Rodney King Shot While Riding Bike." *Los Angeles Times.* November 30, 2007. http://articles.latimes.com/2007/nov/30/local/me-king30.

Salem, D'Jamila. "Canceled Events." *Los Angeles Times.* May 1, 1992. http://articles.latimes.com/1992-05-01/local/me-1519_1_los-angeles.

———. "King Case Aftermath: A City in Crisis." *Los Angeles Times.* May 2, 1992. http://articles.latimes.com/1992-05-02/local/me-1338_1_weekend-cancellations.

Serrano, Richard A. "Upset and Unglued, King Stays Behind a Locked Door." *Los Angeles Times.* May 1, 1992. http://articles.latimes.com/1992-05-01/news/mn-1398_1_angela-king.

Stewart, Sally Ann. "King Case Still Taking Its Toll." *USA Today.* June 2, 1994. http://www.time.com/time/specials/2007/la_riot/0,28757,1614117,00.html #ixzz1e4w33800.

TMZ. "Forget Getting Along—Let's Box!" September 14, 2009. http://www.tmz.com/2009/09/14/rodney-king-boxing-photos/#.TsaVh0aQrA0.

———. "Rodney King's Been Shot!" November 29, 2007. http://www.tmz.com/2007/11/29/rodney-kings-been-shot/#.TsaWMkaQrA0.

UCLA Film and Television Archive. "The Rodney King Case and the Los Angeles Uprising." http://old.cinema.ucla.edu/pdfs/RK_LA.pdf.

United States v. Koon, Powell, Wind, and Briseno, 833 F. Supp. 769; 1993 U.S. Dist. LEXIS 17926.

University of Missouri–Kansas City School of Law. "LAPD Officers' Trials: A Chronology." *Famous American Trials.* http://law2.umkc.edu/faculty/projects/ftrials/lapd/lapd.html.

University of Southern California. "The Los Angeles Riots, 1992." *Special Collections Department.* http://www.usc.edu/libraries/archives/la/la_riot.html.

Wallace, Amy, and David Ferrell. "Verdicts Greeted with Outrage and Disbelief." *Los Angeles Times.* April 30, 1992. http://articles.latimes.com/1992-04-30/news/mn-1888_1_los-angeles.

Warren, Jenifer. "Verdicts Spark Protests, Violence Across California." *Los Angeles Times.* May 01, 1992. http://articles.latimes.com/1992-05-01/news/mn-1251_1_bay-bridge.

Warren, Jenifer, and Martha Groves. "Verdicts Spark Protests, Violence Across California." *Los Angeles Times.* May 01, 1992. http://articles.latimes.com/1992-05-01/news/mn-1399_1_san-francisco-state-university.

Weintraub, Daniel M. "Guard Action Delayed by Organization Glitches." *Los Angeles Times.* May 01, 1992. http://articles.latimes.com/1992-05-01/news/mn-1415_1_national-guard.

YouTube. "Bob Meloni vs Rodney King Celebrity Boxing 11/20/2009." Uploaded by larryspera on November 21, 2009. http://www.youtube.com/watch?v=LDzXdUiPe8I.

———. "Celebrity Boxing 11—Justice and Payback—Rodney King vs. Simon 'The Renegade' Aouad." Uploaded by Gofightlive on September 23, 2009. http://www.youtube.com/watch?feature=fvwp&v=bPwPhNeoOx0&NR=1.